Celebrating Diversity in the Language Classroom

Selected Papers from the 1998 Central States Conference

Edited by

Aleidine J. Moeller
University of Nebraska—Lincoln

Associate Editors

Kathryn A. Corl
The Ohio State University

Rita Ricaurte
Nebraska Wesleyan University

Authors

Jayne Abrate
José Felipe Acosta
Scott Barkhurst
Judith W. Failoni
Gerhard Fischer
Carol Galvin Flood
Sarah Gendron
Paige Gilbert
Kathleen Hajek
Thomas Lovik
Patrick McConeghy

Heather D. Mendoza
Elizabeth Mittman
Patricia Paulsell
Linda Paulus
George Peters
Susanne Rott
Emily Spinelli
Joan F. Turner
Margaret Wendling
Kathleen Wheatley
Deborah Wilburn Robinson

National Textbook Company
a division of NTC/CONTEMPORARY PUBLISHING GROUP
Lincolnwood, Illinois USA

Publisher: Steve VanThournout
Editorial Director: Cindy Krejcsi
Executive Editor: Mary Jane Maples
Editor: Berkeley L. Frank
Director, World Languages Publishing: Keith Fry
Art Director: Ophelia M. Chambliss
Production Manager: Margo Goia

ISBN: 0-8442-0428-5

Review and Acceptance Procedures
Central States Conference Report

The CSC Report is a refereed volume of selected papers from the annual Central States Conference on the Teaching of Foreign Languages. The procedures by which articles are reviewed and accepted for publication begin with the submission of a proposal and abstract to present a session at the Central States Conference. The members of the annual program committee read and evaluate each proposal and abstract.

After the proposals have been evaluated and the sessions selected, presenters are contacted by the editor and invited to submit an article for consideration for publication in the Report. Copies of the publication guidelines are sent to the presenters who indicate an interest in submitting for publication. Prospective authors then submit six copies of their manuscript along with a diskette.

All articles are read and evaluated by at least five persons: the editor, the two associate editors, and at least four members of the editorial board of reviewers. Before articles are sent to the associate editors and reviewers, the names and affiliations of the authors are removed to help ensure a fair evaluation. Normally, articles are sent to reviewers who have expertise in the area treated in the article. The reviewers are asked to make one of three recommendations: (1) publish as is; (2) publish after revising/rewriting; (3) do not publish.

After the recommendations from the reviewers are returned, the editor makes the final decision about whether or not to publish the article. Thus, at least six different people read and evaluate the article before it is selected to appear in the Report.

1998 CSC Report Editorial Board

Reviewers

Terry Ballman	University of Northern Colorado
James E. Becker	University of Northern Iowa
Jodi Benton	University of Nebraska—Lincoln
Robert Godwin-Jones	Virginia Tech University
Marilyn Gordon	Fremont Public Schools (NE)
Tony Houston	University of Nebraska—Lincoln
Pamela LeZotte	University of Nebraska—Lincoln
Joseph McClanahan	University of Nebraska—Lincoln
Takako McCrann	University of Nebraska—Lincoln
Joyce Michaelis	Nebraska Wesleyan University
Christel Ortmann	University of Nebraska—Lincoln
Marie Trayer	Millard Public Schools (NE)
Gabrielle Valenciano	University of Nebraska—Lincoln
Donna VanHandle	Mt. Holyoke University
Sharon Watts	Omaha Public Schools

Preface

For its thirtieth annual meeting, the Central States Conference on the Teaching of Foreign Languages returned to the site of its very first conference in 1969—Milwaukee, Wisconsin. The theme of the Conference, Celebrating Diversity, was originally inspired by Milwaukee's rich ethnic diversity. However, as the theme developed, it became evident that foreign language educators are surrounded by diversity. From our students' preferred learning styles to their varied backgrounds, from the delivery methods and approaches we use to teach our courses, to the activities we use in class, diversity is an integral part of the foreign language teaching profession. Regardless of the language we teach, we are often seen as the experts on diversity in our communities.

Not surprisingly, the Conference program reflected the theme of diversity. On Thursday, language immersion workshops were conducted in French, German, Japanese, and Spanish as well as two all-day workshops and sixteen half-day workshops. The 160 sessions on Friday and Saturday embraced the theme of diversity on such topics as dialects of Spanish, relating to gay and lesbian students, and activities for students with learning disabilities. Three focus sessions dealt with adapting instruction and curriculum to the learner, the changing demographics in our schools and on our campuses, and immersion foreign language programs.

Technology sessions showcased teaching with the Web and explored the effect technology has on learners in the foreign language experience. The integration of National Standards and state frameworks in the classroom was the focus of the Extension Workshop and numerous sessions.

The Conference was highlighted by two outstanding speakers. Dr. Stephen Krashen, the keynote speaker at the plenary session following the annual Awards luncheon, spoke on "Free Voluntary Reading: The Answer to the Transitions Problem." Dr. Robert DiDonato addressed the Conference Luncheon on "Reviewing and Reassessing Language Instruction."

Due to the historic nature of the Conference, the thirtieth annual meeting of the Central States Conference, a special effort was made to encourage the founders to attend in order that they might be recognized for their contributions at special events during the Conference. Returning home to Milwaukee gave the Central States Conference an opportunity to reflect on how the profession has changed over the last 30 years and to pay tribute to those individuals, who 30 years ago, had the vision and stamina to bring into being the Central States Conference on the Teaching of Foreign Languages.

Karen Cardenas
1998 Conference Chair

Contents

Virtual Classrooms: Diversifying Instruction

Learning Styles and Effective Language Learning Strategies

Introduction
Celebrating Diversity in the Language Classroom

Aleidine J. Moeller
University of Nebraska—Lincoln

The Central States Conference theme for 1998 focuses on the issue of diversity in foreign language education. The increased linguistic and cultural diversity of U.S. society has significantly impacted the student makeup of the classroom and the teaching of foreign languages. Teachers today face the challenge of teaching gifted, at risk, handicapped, and ethnically diverse students in one classroom. Creating an effective learning environment for students of diverse cultural, ethnic, and racial backgrounds where second language learning is optimal has become the focus of numerous research studies, professional journals, the National Foreign Language Standards, and in sessions and conference workshops in recent years.

The eleven articles in this volume address the issue of celebrating diversity in the foreign language classroom from myriad perspectives. The four major categories reflect recent innovations and research designed to assist teachers of foreign languages in creating a classroom environment that is meaningful, relevant, and inclusive of all learners.

Virtual Classroom: Diversifying Instruction

In the first section of the Report, Jayne Abrate illustrates how communicative activities can be linked to authentic cultural content via the WWW. The WWW as a source of cultural information combined with peer interaction about topics of mutual interest allows the foreign language learner to go beyond the typical materials in textbooks and the limitations of documents that are beyond the abilities of students to interpret knowledgeably without extensive direction and explanation. Abrate offers an example of project teaching related to holidays to illustrate how the Web can be used to promote culture and language skills in and outside the classroom walls.

Emily Spinelli and Carol Galvin Flood provide guidelines and generic exercise types for integrating WWW materials into the Spanish classroom.

Strategies for facilitating reading of WWW materials are provided as well as model activities that can be easily replicated by classroom teachers for their language and culture purposes.

Gerhard Fischer ties the National Standards to classroom instruction by creating a virtual classroom through an e-mail correspondence between a German classroom in Wisconsin and one in Germany. Fischer found that not only did this project facilitate communication among the participants, but, more importantly, it promoted the building of communities through communication. This two year e-mail project serves as the basis for insights regarding potential benefits of e-mail integration in the foreign language classroom.

Learning Styles and Effective Language Learning Strategies

In this section Linda Paulus, Kathleen Hajek, and José Felipe Acosta investigate two important questions: (1) how to encourage the maximum use of comprehensible input in the classroom and (2) how to establish when English is necessary. The ability to provide a sustained flow of comprehensible input and to get students to attend to that input are skills highly desirable in language learners. These authors provide elaborate techniques for developing strategic competence to promote communicative skills in foreign language learners.

Suzanne Rott and Margaret Wendling focus on the use of compensation strategies within the framework of communicative language teaching. They argue that the linguistically challenging environment of the communicative classroom makes it critical that learners be taught compensation strategies to "minimize linguistic impasses and prevent communication breakdown." The authors identify compensation strategies for reading, writing, oral, and listening tasks and suggest applications for daily lesson plans as well as for testing.

Teaching Culture: A Context for Diversity

In this section Scott Barkhurst and Judith Failoni describe and demonstrate the concept of meaningful extra-curricular activities and how language learning and cultural literacy can be evaluated in a nontraditional setting. The interdisciplinary French project described in this article uses the performing arts as a learning tool. This approach to the teaching of language and culture through the presentation of a theatrical performance is complete with an authentic meal, music, and dance. The theory of Multiple Intelligences serves as the psychological basis for this multi-sensory approach as it accommodates diverse learning styles and special needs.

Sarah Gendron and Paige Gilbert illustrate the benefits of using music and theater in the language classroom as a way to create a cultural context of the second language culture so that learners can become aware of cultural references. Music and theater allow the students to "live" the language in ways that would not otherwise be possible within the limits of the university classroom. The authors describe and illustrate how music and theater can be integrated into the beginning and intermediate-level language courses in a relatively fixed curriculum in order to provide beginning and intermediate language learners a more direct link to the target culture.

Joan Turner and Heather Mendoza have produced a model of language instruction that combines principles of cognitive psychology, content-enriched instruction, and communicative language teaching based on an aspect of pop culture. In the context of the movie *Evita,* the authors designed a sample teaching unit based on the life of Evita making use of film, music, and print designed to provide a method for motivating students while increasing their linguistic capabilities and heightening their cultural awareness. The authors tie the unit to the National Standards for communication.

Preparing Teachers and Designing Curriculum for Diversity

The German faculty at Michigan State University (Thomas Lovik, Patrick McConeghy, Elizabeth Mittman, Patricia Paulsell, George Peters,) decided in 1992 to integrate issues of diversity and multiculturalism in the context of German Studies into their undergraduate German language curriculum. The curriculum includes discussions of various issues relating to the presence of ethnic minorities in Germany—from historical perspectives, to social and political realities, to cultural manifestation—at every stage of the student's progress through the program. The article conveys how this works in practice and illustrates how individual instructors at each level of the undergraduate program attempt to realize this goal. Such a commitment to restructuring curriculum and instruction in order to diversify foreign language instruction makes foreign language a more realistic and relevant course of study for our undergraduates. This program can serve as a model for other colleges and universities in addressing the issue of diversity.

Deborah Wilburn Robinson reports on the formation of a Foreign and Second Language Professional Development network designed as a partnership between the universities and K-12 schools (Professional Development Schools). A research study was conducted to seek input from schools to better inform the establishment of the school-university partnership. Such a professional partner school model will combine preservice and inservice education in a school-based model that will better prepare foreign language educators to deal with the challenges of educating K-12 learners.

Kathleen Wheatley posits that the tendency to teach a standard dialect of a language can ignore the rich diversity that exists in the language. It is her view that "if we are truly committed to celebrating diversity, then the study of dialects should be a component of our curriculum." In her article she provides examples of language variation in Spanish and examines the historical development of the variations as well as their impact on the language.

1
Using the World Wide Web Communicatively to Explore Another Culture

Jayne Abrate
Southern Illinois University at Carbondale

Culture and the Web

Sharing cultural knowledge with speakers of the target language via the World Wide Web (WWW) provides language students with the opportunity to present their own culture, learn firsthand about another, and interact in a spirit of discovery with their counterparts in a foreign culture. The WWW represents a valuable informational resource for the foreign language class which teachers should utilize and train their students to use effectively. As Seelye states: "The basic aim of a communication class is to have the student learn to communicate with people from the foreign culture" (1984: 23). However, limiting the WWW to use as a reference tool ignores its vast potential for interactivity and as a facilitator of possibilities for communication that extends far beyond the restrictive textual exchanges of electronic mail. Students can certainly use the WWW to transmit e-mail (Knight 1994; Abrate 1994; Suozzo 1995), but they can also post formatted written documents, images, sound, and video which their correspondents in other countries can consult. Research has shown that "students are willing and even eager to get online with native or nonnative speakers to communicate informally in the target language" (Underwood and Kelm cited by Beauvois 1997). By linking communicative activities to authentic cultural content, students can use their language skills to explore in depth other subjects, knowledge of which will further enhance their overall linguistic competence.

As a source of cultural information the WWW is unparalleled in its offerings of up-to-date news, art images, illustrations and maps, literary and historical documents, advice for tourists to name only a few, but, in many cases, the thoroughness with which topics or geographical areas are treated remains sporadic. Furthermore, posted materials concerning less tangible areas such as values and beliefs or daily life are scarce. One occasionally finds references to religious practices or the role of women in a given culture, for example, but in order to understand and appreciate cultural differences, students need sufficient context to make reasonable assumptions and the opportunity to ask questions to confirm or refine their conclusions. Robinson-Stuart and Nocon refer to culture as "a process, that is, as a way of perceiving, interpreting, feeling, being in the world. . .This perspective views culture as part of the process of living and being in the world, the part that is necessary for making meaning" (1996: 432). Permitting American students to interact with peers in the target culture on topics relevant to their lives and interests leads them beyond both the typical, often anecdotal, materials found in textbooks and the limitations of documents that are frequently beyond the abilities of students to interpret knowledgeably without extensive direction and explanation. Short of visiting the country, such guided exploration offers students a more nuanced look at another way of life than would otherwise be possible in a classroom with a textbook.

The rapidity with which messages can be sent and responded to constitutes a fundamental attraction of electronic communication. Certainly, e-mail correspondence projects provide a venue for discussing issues of interest, asking questions, and obtaining reliable answers, but the use of the WWW permits students to share photographs and other illustrations such as handwriting samples, drawings, flyers, posters, programs, schoolwork, or other realia and even include spoken greetings, songs, and other recordings. In particular, WWW users can now post video documents. Given the revolution in WWW technology that has occurred in just months, it is likely that all these possibilities and more will become generally available in the foreseeable future.

Technology Requirements and Advantages

The first requirement for planning a project such as the one described here is access to a WWW server where documents can be posted. Universities generally have several servers, and a language department might even have its own. More and more secondary schools and school districts have servers, and commercial Web providers also offer space for housing documents. Preparing text and graphics or illustrations for posting on the WWW can be done by anyone. Editors such as the one in Netscape Gold (http://www.netscape.com/) function just like a word processor, and, in fact, many word processing programs now have features which automatically format text in the HTML language used on the WWW. Digitizing illustrations requires only a scanner equipped with software such as Photoshop (http:///www.adobe.com/) which can save the image in the .jpg or .gif formats of the WWW. Digital 35mm cameras, which store and download already digitized images directly to the computer, can be found at more and more reasonable prices. Any teacher can quickly learn to prepare text and scan images for posting to the WWW using equipment that is available in many schools and certainly in the community at local libraries or universities, for example.

Audio and video documents remain, for the moment, more complicated to post, if not to prepare. A multimedia computer equipped with appropriate software and a microphone permits the digitizing of sound files, and digital video cameras store and download video images.[1] The main hindrance is the space required to download and store the huge files associated with these applications. They can consume valuable space on the WWW server, and many schools do not yet have a rapid enough connection speed to the WWW to make their use feasible. In certain instances, teachers may also have the option of setting up a discussion group or chat room exclusively for the students involved. Just as the capacity for nearly instantaneous message transmission first offered by electronic mail made written communication come alive for students, the WWW can do the same for audio-visual exchanges. With CUSeeMe, students can participate in real time video exchanges. A small video camera is attached directly to the computer, and the signals are transmitted digitally. In addition, certain technical difficulties of traditional e-mail and video exchanges are minimized by the WWW browsers. Even with minimal technical facilities, sending messages via the browser's e-mail function circumvents the problems of accents[2] which can also be displayed with no problem in WWW documents. Finally, group correspondence presents other advantages such as compensating for differences in the number of male and female students or variations in age and, most importantly, can involve all students in using the technology. While a lab where each student can have access to the WWW is ideal, many of these suggestions can be implemented with even with minimal facilities. The cultural and communicative nature of these activities keeps the focus on content rather than on the technology itself.

Oral and written interaction with native informants concerning a well-defined subject can facilitate communication and encourage the give and take of real dialogue. The asynchronous communication of e-mail and WWW exchanges frees students from the anxiety of speaking: "The rapidity of student-teacher interactions and the relative ease with which they are conducted contribute to the feeling of hybrid communication—somewhere between writing and speaking" (Beauvois 1997: 172). Many common cultural topics do not require extensive knowledge beyond what students already possess or can easily acquire, and projects involving holidays, schoolwork or schedules, towns or states, sports events, youth activities, regional heritage, or current events can easily be created either for a one-time exchange or for an ongoing project and can be adapted so that students of all ages and skill levels can benefit. To locate a class in the target culture willing to participate in a class correspondence project, teachers can consult various WWW sites including the AATF (http://aatf.utsa.edu/), AATG (http://www.aatg.org/), and AATSP (http://www.aatsp.org/home.html). If a teacher already has a colleague with whom he or she already corresponds by regular mail or e-mail, that teacher may be inspired to learn about the WWW.[3]

Project-Based Teaching on the Web

The cooperating teachers must first determine in which language the project will be carried out. Since both development of the local WWW site and examination of the other group's work can involve significant class time, use of the target language should be encouraged whenever possible while keeping in mind the advantages of and need for fruitful collaboration. For the purposes of these examples, it is assumed that the presentation phase will occur in the target language and subsequent discussion will take place in the language of the document being considered. In other words, students will present their own culture and respond to questions or comments about it in the target language and will examine the target culture and ask questions about it in their own language. In determining the tasks to be accomplished and the language in which they will be performed, teachers should consider (1) the goals of both classes (for instance, a target language class could conceivably be paired with a native language class of social studies or geography instead of a class studying their language); (2) the communicative tasks envisioned, either presentational, consultative, or interactive; (3) the feasibility, given content, instructional level, and technical facilities, to carry out the project; (4) and the wishes of the corresponding teacher and class. However, these decisions are admittedly arbitrary and will vary according to the age and linguistic ability of the classes involved.

Communicating actively via the WWW allows teachers to address the national standards in a way few other pedagogical tools do. *Standards for Foreign Language Learning: Preparing for the 21st Century* establishes five goal areas: Communication, Cultures, Connections, Comparisons, and Communities. WWW exchanges between classes and individuals give students the opportunity to practice interpersonal, interpretive, and presentational modes of **communication** in the target language. It provides them with immediate access to current authentic documents from the target **culture(s)** as well as a heretofore unavailable cadre of native informants. The wealth of information students can locate on the WWW concerning nearly any topic permits them to **connect** with other disciplines in a structured way as a class and in a very individualized manner as well. In order for students to make **comparisons** between the target language and culture and their own, they will probably require significantly more guidance from the teacher than in the other goal areas, but again the richness and immediacy of WWW materials and interchange facilitate this process. Finally, WWW technology gives students both the possibility and the incentive to participate in the target language in **communities** far beyond the classroom. In many schools, teachers would be hard-pressed to address some of these goals without access to WWW technology.

The presentational aspect of posting documents on the WWW encourages students to do research, interpret and summarize relevant details, organize their findings in the text they compose, and illustrate it with pictures, drawings, or other visual images. Lafford and Lafford point out that online technologies "...provide an engaging environment for real use of the language. In the progression from reading and fact-finding to real communication (both in writing and speaking to others) and in writing up one's experiences with these activities, the students are using the language" (1997: 259). If facilities permit, they can develop sound and/or video support for the initial presentation which can range from recorded greetings, spoken texts, songs, dialogues, or skits to video recordings of events that take place in the school or community. These are then formatted and posted on the WWW, either for general consumption or in a hidden directory known only to a corresponding class. Composing documents in the target language should not become a translation activity but, insofar as possible, an adaptation of material to the target language; this forces students to consider carefully the message and intended audience—which ideas cannot be easily translated and must be explained and illustrated, which aspects of a topic will most interest the other class, how students can present both the positive and negative sides of an issue in order to give a balanced portrayal. Translation too often leads students to focus on finding a one-to-one equivalent rather than on conveying an idea.

A well-structured preparatory stage involving analysis and description of the native culture which goes beyond free research and composition and leads students to consider their foreign peers' interests and reactions lays the groundwork for serious cultural comparison. Many teachers subscribe to the "... mistaken assumption that language study and performance per se will automatically open the door to another culture and to shared understanding, without any specific treatments designed to promote intercultural understanding and interaction" (Robinson-Stuart and Nocon 1996: 433). Insofar as their cognitive and linguistic skills allow, students should consider not only the cultural events or objects they describe and illustrate, but the historical or ethnic perspective, underlying assumptions, related issues, and the social ramifications of a particular behavior or tradition. For instance, consideration of a holiday could include discussion of how the celebration began, how it has evolved and why (advent of television, increased commercialism, more working parents, involvement of the schools), as well as the implications of the event for society as a whole (recognition of various ethnic groups or legal decisions connected with the holiday).

Analyses of multicultural and cross-cultural communication and methodologies are readily available in the literature (Kramsch 1993; Seeyle 1984; Robinson 1988; Steele and Suozzo 1994; Valdes 1986), but for the teacher attempting to develop student awareness of cultural phenomena and the ability to make informed comparisons between their culture and the target culture, particularly at early levels of instruction, one effective approach is to use directed questioning. By reaching beyond the item or event being studied to consider the who, what, when, where, why, and how of it, teachers can lead their students to become better observers and perhaps to express informed judgments or simply not to judge, rather than jumping to the stereotypical conclusions which seem almost an inevitable consequence of exposure to another culture. Solid preparation leads students to observe and analyze the culture rather than merely reacting to it.

Although there are not always answers to all of these questions, important considerations in preparing a document might include:

1. How or why did the event or tradition begin? When, and where?
2. Are certain legends or beliefs associated with it?
3. Are there related religious, ethnic, patriotic, regional, or social issues?
4. What underlying values or beliefs influence this event or tradition?
5. Have problems or criticisms been associated with it?
6. Who participates and how? Is it widespread or local?
7. What outward manifestations or objects are associated with it?
8. What are your personal views about this event or tradition?
9. How do your family, classmates, school officials, other townspeople view it?

Such questions provide a structure which can accommodate the results of research, family and local experiences and observations, as well as personal opinion.

When both classes have posted documents on the WWW, the corresponding group can study them for cultural content, linguistic accuracy, and comparisons to the home culture. Problems with clarity of presentation as well as usage will naturally give rise to questions which can be directed via e-mail to the authors for clarification or revision of the WWW documents or continued e-mail discussion. The spirit of friendly communication and even competition fostered during the creation of materials gives an incentive for students to communicate accurately and enthusiastically.

The exchanges between classes related to the documents posted depends greatly on the facilities available for individual student use. WWW browsers offer an e-mail function that guarantees compatibility for the sending and receiving of accented messages, and WWW pages should always include a "mail to" link which allows users to click on it and send a message while viewing the page. Active electronic correspondence between students depends on external factors such as whether students can individually use computers to send mail and if they have their own e-mail addresses, for instance, as well as on the facilities available to the other class. If student access is limited to one computer in the classroom, it will be more time-consuming to send individual messages, although not impossible. If only one e-mail address is used, it is harder to pair specific students. Of course, individual messages can still be sent and answered, but the time factor of pairing individuals as opposed to group responses must be weighed against the pedagogical benefits.

The types of project can easily be adapted to whatever time is allotted, the interests and abilities of the participants, and the technical facilities available. They can be limited to a short, one-time group effort or expanded to encompass a multifaceted project covering several interrelated themes and lasting the entire school year. In fact, Mantle Bromley's assertion that ". . . the frequency of [inter-ethnic] contact was directly related to the improvement" (1992: 121) in attitudes argues for a more extended project. Similarly, the analysis and comparison which occurs can be as involved and structured as the level of the students and desires of the teachers permit. The following two themes, holidays and the local community, illustrate how specific features of the WWW can enhance both communication skills and cultural awareness.

Holidays: A Context for Culture

Holidays provide a wealth of subject matter which can generate interest and excitement throughout the year. Halloween offers a contrast between celebrations that can spark students' interest and effectively launch a long-term project. The American celebration complete with costumes, haunted houses, and trick or treating can be presented through explanatory texts relating the history of the holiday, problems associated with it such as the dangers involved, the tricks played, or religious objections, and how it has evolved over the years; accompanying illustrations can include photographs of typical skeleton, ghost, or witch costumes, decorations in the school or in front of people's homes, or instructions for carving a jack-o-lantern.[4] Students might record descriptions of their costumes and how they will celebrate. A video might show a school costume parade, a hay ride, a haunted house, students trick or treating, or a demonstration of how to carve a jack-o-lantern. At the same time, the lack of comparable festivities in most other countries will surprise students, particularly as their keypals present more somber traditions and activities associated with honoring the dead on All Saints' Day, a holiday more comparable to American Memorial Day observances.

A sample timeline for a more involved project might include:

Week 1:   Students brainstorm a list of Halloween/All Saints' Day traditions and icons.

Weeks 2-3: Individual students or small groups research these traditions and icons.

Weeks 4-6: Students prepare and organize the content of the WWW page in the target language.

Weeks 7-8: Students select illustrations and, if appropriate, audio or video documents.

Week 9:   Material is posted on the WWW.

Weeks 10-12: Students consult and compare. They correspond with their counterparts and revise the WWW site as necessary.

Certainly, this structure can be modified in any number of ways to accommodate other topics, more regular presentation and exchange of documents, and, simply, teacher preference. A topic such as food and eating habits, for example, would be more conducive to less-involved regular postings and written exchanges. The flexibility of such a project to respond to individual interests makes this technology ideal for communicative, interactive activities on cultural topics.

Thanksgiving represents another American tradition that can serve equally well to stimulate discussion and cultural comparisons. Students prepare textual or audio-visual documents on the origin of Thanksgiving illustrated with images of Pilgrim costumes and typical decorations, offer menus and recipes accompanied by pictures of the dishes and a table, and describe individual family celebrations. Audio recordings of Thanksgiving songs or poems might also be included, while video footage might record a Thanksgiving pageant or parade. Although other countries, with the exception of Canada, do not celebrate this holiday, there may be comparable harvest festivals or feast days that combine some elements of American Thanksgiving. In spite of the fact that most of the presentation is on the American side for this holiday, the questions and comments evoked will no doubt prove enlightening to the American students, and the other class can reciprocate by describing a holiday in the target culture that has no American equivalent.

Christmas constitutes one of the holidays richest in traditions the world over. If consideration of religious holidays is problematic, New Year's celebrations provide a ready substitute. Consideration of the secular and religious aspects of the Christmas season reveals aspects of American culture, such as the emphasis on commercialism, often to the exclusion of any religious focus, or the parallel celebrations of Hanukkah or Kwanza. Written descriptions along with illustrations of public decorations, store displays in October, Santa Claus surrounded by his elves and reindeer, Christmas lighting on individual homes, and Christmas parades as well as Christmas carols sung by the students or video of a Christmas play or children seeing Santa Claus can all be transmitted via the WWW. Differences in gift giving, typical holiday meals and when they are eaten, religious observances, or the American penchant for Christmas lights offer many contrasts to more subdued or less secular celebrations in other countries.

Holidays offer a nearly endless source of cultural information that can readily involve related topics ranging from food to friendship to family to religion to politics. The community also provides another means for students to present themselves to others with a wide range of options and themes. Students can create or adapt many documents available locally for WWW presentation to their keypals. These might include:

1. texts recounting the town's history, profiling noteworthy citizens, describing its geography or unique features, highlighting local industries;

2. descriptive brochures, flyers, or posters with images and text;

3. a video guided tour or narrated images which students prepare and conduct of local monuments, city hall, the fire station;

4. photographs of people working, construction crews, school bus drivers, crossing guards, firemen, waiters;

5. interviews with local dignitaries, the mayor or a city council member, the local historian, president of the Rotary Club, a member of the clergy, a school board member;

6. a map of important sites;

7. photographs or videos of houses or neighborhoods typical of the town's architecture;

8. illustrations, publicity information, or videos of local festivals, cultural events, or other celebrations;

9. information on what is available to do locally, such as sports facilities, clubs or groups one can join;

10. information on local government, laws, or customs.

This sort of presentation can expand to include the surrounding region or state and represents a truly comprehensive subject ripe for comparison because the other class can respond point for point to the features highlighted. The same preparatory and comparative questions mentioned previously can serve to guide the students' efforts so that they derive the maximum benefit from the exchange of information and commentary.

Once the presentational documents are posted, students will then work with them to learn about the other culture and take advantage of opportunities to communicate. The exercises and activities that teachers develop can range from traditional non-WWW applications to highly interactive, technologically based parallel or extension activities. Numerous WWW sites exist (see Appendix) which offer examples of pedagogical applications of WWW materials and, in particular, offer advice on creating teaching materials which take full advantage of the WWW's capabilities (http://www.mndc.fandm. edu/TBA/Create_TBA.html). At lower levels, students might search for responses to specific questions, complete form-type exercises, or participate in a WWW scavenger hunt, and as students' proficiency increases, the tasks they are asked to perform become more complex, such as summarizing information found on the WWW, performing their own subject searches, or independently preparing material for posting. In a like manner, assessment techniques must be coordinated with the exercises and activities chosen. The communicative WWW project described in this article lends itself particularly well to portfolio assessment if the students prepare their materials in the target language and evaluate their cultural observation and analysis skills. Their understanding of their counterparts' cultural presentations as well as their e-mail messages can be evaluated for linguistic content and accuracy. However, it is crucial to fostering communication that their messages not be judged per se. Knowing a message might be graded is almost certain to inhibit communication. Rather a composite text representative of the language used by several students should be adapted for evaluative purposes. Students might correct errors or paraphrase a sample message, or they might transform a text based on a particular grammar point (rewriting in the past or as another person, for example). In short, the exercises and activities used in such a project to communicate as well as to evaluate correspond to typical techniques teachers already use. However, the interactivity of the WWW and the unique resources available allow emphasis to be placed on the kind of communicative tasks, observation of authentic cultural documents, and individualized activities that are most difficult to incorporate in a traditional classroom.

Conclusion

Ultimately, a WWW class exchange carries the benefit of regular mail correspondence projects several steps further. Suozzo states:

> It is essential that we. . . attempt to bridge the vast distances separating our students from the cultures they are studying, to remind them that learning another language and cultures is above all an ongoing effort at communication with others. . . . E-mail offers us one major possibility of achieving the intimacy of communication that binds people of different cultures to one another (1995: 85).

By combining a rapid transfer of messages with the audio-visual support of WWW documents, students can experience not only the sights and sounds of the target culture but interact with native speakers of the target language of the same age and with similar interests—truly the next best thing to being there. As Bush explains: "The use of new technologies ... creates experiences that are extremely compelling and motivational for those language learners fortunate enough to have the experience" (1997: 288). Certainly, such a project requires the availability of technical support, both hardware and the skills necessary to create and post materials, but as more and more schools are equipping themselves with the technology, a project such as this provides the means to involve language students in exchanges that extend far beyond the school's walls, allow them to make new friends, and encourage them to learn more about themselves and the world around them.

Notes

Since the technical specifications for transferring WWW documents to a server vary from place to place, it is best to consult with the local technical advisor or Web provider for instructions.

1. Many of the technical aspects of creating Web pages, digitizing or posting images or audio or video materials, or hardware requirements are beyond the scope of this article. Video documents, in particular, require a very high-speed connection to the WWW to be feasible, but the other types of documents are now staple features of most WWW sites. If the teacher or a knowledgeable student does not possess the necessary expertise, the technical advisor at the school should be able to provide all the information and support necessary. MS Front Page (http://www.microsoft.com/) is a Web page management tool that permits the inclusion of discussion groups and many other interactive features on a Web site. To be able to prepare all the documents and functions mentioned in this article requires a multimedia computer with microphone linked to the WWW, a full-page color scanner, a digital 35mm camera, a digital video camera, a CUSeeMe video camera, and software including a WWW browser and editor, graphics software, and WWW site manager software. At current prices, the abovementioned items can be purchased for under $3500.

2. Many teachers who have tried e-mail correspondence have discovered the pitfalls of using accents with e-mail. In order for accents to be transmitted correctly, each user needs to use compatible, usually the same, e-mail software.

3. Disparities in technical facilities may be a problem in this sort of project. However, many European and Canadian schools have WWW access, and governments are actively promoting inclusion of this technology in instruction. The projects described here could also be modified for a pairing of two classes studying the target language. Such a project would certainly provide increased communicative opportunities and the possibility of developing students' skills of cultural observation and analysis, but the benefits of cultural authenticity would be lost.

4. Permission should always be obtained before posting pictures of individuals or reproducing any copyrighted materials on the WWW.

References

Abrate, Jayne. 1994. "Authentic Communication via Minitel." In *Meeting New Challenges in the Foreign Language Classroom,* ed. Gale K. Crouse. Lincolnwood, IL: National Textbook Co., 79-90.

Beauvois, Margaret Healy. 1997. "Computer-Mediated Communication (CMC): Technology for Improving Speaking and Writing." In *Technology-Enhanced Language Learning,* ed. Michael D. Bush and Robert M. Terry. Lincolnwood, IL: National Textbook Co., pp. 165-84.

Bush, Michael D., and Terry, Robert M., eds. 1997. *Technology-Enhanced Language Learning.* Lincolnwood, IL: National Textbook Co.

Knight, Susan. 1994. "Making Authentic Cultural and Linguistic Connections." *Hispania,* 77,2: 288-94.

Kramsch, Claire. 1993. *Context and Culture in Language Teaching.* Oxford: Oxford University Press.

Lafford, Peter A., and Lafford, Barbara A. 1997. "Learning Language and Culture with Internet Technologies." Pp. 215–62. In *Technology-Enhanced Language Learning,* ed. Michael D. Bush and Robert M. Terry. Lincolnwood, IL: National Textbook Co.

Mantle-Bromley, Corinne. 1992. "Preparing Students for Meaningful Culture Learning." *Foreign Language Annals,* 25,2: 117-27.

National Standards in Foreign Language Education Project. 1996. *Standards for Foreign Language Learning: Preparing for the 21st Century.* Lawrence, KS: Allen Press.

Robinson. Gail. 1988. *Crosscultural Understanding.* New York: Prentice-Hall.

Robinson-Stuart, Gail, and Honorine Nocon. 1996. "Second Culture Acquisition: Ethnography in the Foreign Language Classroom." *Modern Language Journal,* 80,4: 431-49.

Seelye, H. Ned. 1984. *Teaching Culture.* Lincolnwood, IL: National Textbook Co.

Steele, Ross, and Suozzo, Andrew. 1994. *Teaching French Culture: Theory and Practice.* Lincolnwood, IL: National Textbook Co.

Suozzo, Andrew. 1995. "Dialogue and Immediacy in Cultural Instruction: The E-Mail Option." *French Review,* 69,1: 78-87.

Valdes, Joyce Merrill, ed. 1986. *Culture Bound: Bridging the Cultural Gap in Language Teaching.* Cambridge, England: Cambridge University Press.

Appendix
Web Sites for Pedagogy

AATF Teaching with Internet FAQ offers information on finding keypals, samples of Internet and WWW activities, and links to many useful sites [http://aatf.utsa.edu/twiafaq.html]

AATF Commission on Cultural Competence Web site offers links to cultural documents in seven categories (geography, values, literature and the arts, history, social institutions, communication in cultural context, and social patterns and conventions), as well as sample WWW activities, and a guide to learning to navigate the WWW [http://www.siu.edu/~aatf/help.html]

AATG Technology Training Workshops page displays documents created during the workshops in 1997 [http://www.aatg.org/techwss.html]

AATG Links page gives links to many other useful Web sites [http://www.aatg.org/link.html#Ex]

AATG Web Workshop: Building German Studies Sites has many helpful ideas for creating WWW activities as well as samples [http://www.uncg.edu/~lixlpurc/publications/GerWebEx.html]

French Civilisation gives many multimedia modules for the teaching of French civilization created by Marie Ponterio [http://www.cortland.edu/flteach/civ/]

Le Quartier fran(ais du village plan(taire application page, created by Janice Paulsen, offers suggestions for useful WWW documents and accompanying activities [http://www.richmond.edu/~jpaulsen/pedagogy2.html]

Teaching with the Web has links to many language-specific activities on the WWW [http://polyglot.lss.wisc.edu/lss/lang/teach.html#spec]

WWW Notebook for Teachers of French provides this thematic index of French and Francophone cultural activities [http://www.has.vcu.edu/flm/faculty/smoore/index.html]

2
Language, Culture, and the World Wide Web
A Guide for the Preparation and Use of Materials

Emily Spinelli
Carol Galvin Flood
University of Michigan—Dearborn

The potential for the use of the Internet and the World Wide Web as curricular tools for teachers and learners of second languages is today widely recognized. In the past several years numerous articles have been published that discuss the World Wide Web and provide information on how to access it and how to use it for teaching languages. Fidelman (1996) provides a detailed introduction and explanation about the WWW as a pedagogical tool for the language classroom. In addition to dealing with the basics of the WWW, such as logging on, Walz (1997) offers suggestions about using the WWW as a tool for the development of cross-cultural skills. Lafford and Lafford (1997) provide further information about how to teach culture through the Internet. Other articles list and describe Web sites that are relevant to second language teaching. Finnemann's (1996) article offers a basic but extremely useful list of Web sites for second language teaching, including ESL. Rosenzweig (1996) provides a list, organized by theme or topic, of useful Web sites for teachers of Spanish while Abrate (1997) offers a similar list of Web sites for teachers of French.

Despite the fact that the potential of the Internet and the WWW are well known, and despite the fact that there is a wealth of information about how to access the Internet and the World Wide Web, Web site materials are not yet a part of the daily routine in most second language classrooms. The reasons for the failure to incorporate the WWW into the classroom range from a lack of equipment and/or facilities to a lack of knowledge about precisely how to incorporate the materials into the daily lesson plan. It is the purpose of this article to provide guidelines and generic exercise types for including WWW materials into the Spanish classroom on a frequent basis.

Rationale for Using World Wide Web Materials

In her 1992 article, Galloway describes the use of authentic documents to increase student motivation and enhance cultural knowledge. Likewise, Garcia (1991) emphasizes the role that authentic texts play in helping students understand both the target and native culture. Thus, one of the most compelling reasons for using WWW materials in the second language classroom is that they provide an interesting and up-to-date source of authentic materials. Web site materials can complement or substitute for textbook materials by linking to chapter themes and situations. In addition, WWW materials offer the second language instructor the possibility of linking the teaching of language and culture in a variety of ways. WWW materials also provide models of authentic language, facilitate the performance of authentic tasks, and can be used to teach vocabulary and grammar as well as the four language skills: listening, speaking, reading, and writing.[1] Lastly, the use of WWW materials should increase student interest and motivation. In short, the use of WWW materials supports the five C's of the *Standards for Foreign Language Learning* (1997): *communication* (communicate in languages other than English), *cultures* (gain knowledge and understanding of other cultures), *connections* (connect with other disciplines and acquire information), *comparisons* (develop insight into the nature of language and culture), and *communities* (participate in multilingual communities at home and around the world).

Guiding Principles

It must be kept in mind that Web sites are not generally developed for pedagogical purposes. Therefore, most materials must be didacticized in order to make them classroom ready. There are several guiding principles for the preparation of Web site materials for the classroom.

- In order to use Web site materials in the classroom, only the instructor needs to have access to the World Wide Web. It is not necessary to have classroom access via a multimedia projector system or a computer for each student. The Web site materials can be printed out onto a transparency using a color printer; the transparency can then be displayed in the classroom using an overhead projector. If no color printer is available, then the Web site materials can be printed onto regular paper using a black-and-white printer. The materials can then be photocopied so that each student has a copy of the materials.

- Students should perform exercises and activities that simulate what native speakers do with the Web site materials.
- Since Web sites change frequently, instructors will need to be flexible and locate different Web sites to replace those that have disappeared.
- Since the development of effective exercises and activities is time-consuming, instructors need generic exercise formats in order to facilitate the use of Web materials.
- Students should be encouraged to become independent language learners by learning to use the WWW outside of the classroom for learning assigned material and for personal enjoyment.

Basic Guidelines for Preparing and Using WWW Materials

The following basic guidelines have been developed in order to facilitate the preparation of classroom exercises and activities that are based on Web sites. It should be noted that the most productive manner of preparing Web site materials is to locate a site and create the task-based activity for that site. Then work backwards to develop the more mechanical exercises that will prepare students for the task-based activity.

- Select Web sites according to unit/chapter themes and situations.
- For classrooms that do not have access to the Internet and the World Wide Web, print out the Web site material onto a transparency or print out the Web site material onto regular paper and photocopy it for the students.
- Determine why a native speaker would access the site.
- Develop an activity similar to the task a native speaker would perform using the site materials.
- Decide whether to emphasize the speaking or writing skill in the task-based activity. Then decide whether to emphasize the interpersonal, interpretive, or presentational mode.[2]
- Develop lead-in exercises that will help the students read the site materials and also help them perform the task-oriented activity.

Strategies for Facilitating the Reading of WWW Materials

In order to complete exercises and activities developed around a Web site, students must comprehend the information posted at that site. In most situations, the reading skill will be combined with the speaking or writing skill in order to complete the lead-in exercises and task-based activities.

- To develop the reading skill, it is necessary to activate the background knowledge of the students with advance organizers in the form of pre-reading exercises.[3]
  1. Read the title of the Web site and brainstorm topics and ideas to be covered.
  2. Use the accompanying photos, artwork, charts, or tables to brainstorm topics and ideas to be covered. Have students describe the scene of the photos and/or artwork.
  3. Teach or review cognate information:
     a. Spanish -ción = English -tion
        civilización = civilization
        introducción = introduction
     b. Spanish -dad = English -ty
        universidad = university
        publicidad = publicity
  4. Teach or review pertinent vocabulary.
  5. Teach or review pertinent grammar structures.

- Have students learn to read for different purposes such as skimming, scanning, or reading for global comprehension or the gist.
- Have students read with the end task in mind,
- Have students complete an exercise/activity that simulates the task that native speakers would use the Web site for.
  1. Read a weather map to decide what to wear or to decide on an activity.
  2. Read a TV guide to choose a TV program.

Exercises and Activities for the Acquisition of Vocabulary

The following exercises and activities for the acquisition of vocabulary are organized around several generic Web site types including maps, graphs and tables, restaurant menus, and schedules. The exercises are further categorized by the cultural information, language skill, proficiency level, and the Foreign Language Standards addressed. The goal is to provide instructors with exercises and activities that correspond to a particular Web site type so that similar exercises and activities can be easily developed for other sites.[4]

The advantage of using Web site materials as a point of departure for vocabulary acquisition exercises and activities is that the vocabulary is being linked to a meaningful cultural reference. In addition, the vocabulary is being practiced in ways that native speakers would use the same vocabulary items.[5]

GENERIC WEB SITES: Maps: weather maps, city maps, country maps

FOCUS: Vocabulary: weather expressions, numbers, clothing

CULTURE: Geography of Spain: cities, autonomous regions

Climate of Spain

Metric system

SKILL: Speaking

PROFICIENCY LEVEL: Novice

STANDARDS: 1.1   Students engage in conversations, provide and obtain information, express feelings and emotions, and exchange opinions.

1.2   Students understand and interpret written and spoken language on a variety of topics.

2.1   Students demonstrate an understanding of the relationship between the practices and perspectives of the culture studied.

2.2   Students demonstrate an understanding of the relationship between the products and perspectives of the culture studied.

SPECIFIC SITE: Weather map of Spain

URL: http://www.abc.es Pulse: El tiempo

EXERCISES/ACTIVITIES

A. *¿Qué tiempo hace en el norte?* Interpersonal Mode

Students work in pairs. Student 1 has the weather map of Spain. Student 2 has a blank map of Spain. Student 2 asks student 1 what the weather is like in the four areas (north, south, east, and west). Student 1 answers. Student 2 draws in sun/rain/clouds, etc. in the appropriate area of the map. When finished both students check the answers with the weather map.

¿Qué tiempo hace en el norte / oeste / sur / este / centro?

VARIATION 1: Expand vocabulary beyond the basic textbook vocabulary of *Hace sol/frío/calor/fresco* to include the vocabulary listed below the weather map in the key to the symbols.

Está despejado/nuboso/cubierto.

Hay niebla/lluvias/tormentas.

Llueve/nieva.

VARIATION 2:   Use weather maps for other countries of the Spanish-speaking world.

SPECIFIC SITE: Weather map of Spain

URL: http://www.elpais.es Pulse: El tiempo

EXERCISES/ACTIVITIES

A. *¿Qué tiempo hace en Sevilla?* Interpersonal Mode

Students work in pairs. Student 1 has the weather map of Spain. Student 2 has a blank map of Spain. Student 2 asks student 1 what the weather is like in various cities. Student 1 answers. Student 2 draws in sun/rain/clouds, etc. near the cities mentioned on the blank map. When finished both students check the answers with the weather map.

¿Qué tiempo hace en Sevilla / Madrid / Oviedo / Palma de Mallorca / Barcelona / Murcia?

VARIATION 1:   Ask what the weather is like in various autonomous regions of Spain. *¿Qué tiempo hace en Cataluña / Andalucía / Galicia / Castilla-La Mancha / Extremadura ?*

VARIATION 2:   Use weather maps for other countries of the Spanish-speaking world.

B. *¿Cuál es la temperatura en Sevilla?* Interpersonal Mode

Students work in pairs. Student 1 has the weather map of Spain. Student 2 has a blank map of Spain. Student 2 asks student 1 what the high temperature for the day will be in various cities. Student 1 answers. Student 2 writes in the temperature near the city mentioned. When finished student 2 checks the answers with the weather map.

¿Cuál es (será) la temperatura hoy en Sevilla / Madrid / Bilbao / Las Palmas / Valencia / Salamanca / Málaga?

VARIATION 1:   Use weather maps for other countries of the Spanish-speaking world.

FOLLOW-UP ACTIVITY 1: When finished, have students convert or estimate the metric temperatures to Fahrenheit temperatures.

FOLLOW-UP ACTIVITY 2: Have students compare temperatures in major cities of the north/south/east/west with temperatures in the same zones in the U.S.

C. ¿Qué vamos a hacer hoy? Interpretive Mode

Which of the following are appropriate activities today for the various cities listed.

1. *Barcelona / Cádiz / Madrid / Burgos / Toledo*

2. *nadar / comer en un café al aire libre / caminar en el parque / ir a un museo /*

D. ¿Qué debemos ponernos hoy? Interpretive Mode

You are a travel agent in charge of tours around Spain. Today you have tours going to Madrid, Córdoba, Barcelona, Oviedo, and Málaga. Explain to the tourists going to these various cities what they need to wear or carry along in order to be comfortable all day.

GENERIC WEB SITES:	Graphs, tables, family tree
FOCUS:	Vocabulary: family members
CULTURE:	Government of Spain: royal family
SKILL:	Writing
PROFICIENCY LEVEL:	Novice
STANDARDS:	1.1 Students engage in conversations, provide and obtain information, express feelings and emotions, and exchange opinions.
	1.2 Students understand and interpret written and spoken language on a variety of topics.
	2.1 Students demonstrate an understanding of the relationship between the practices and perspectives of the culture studied.
SPECIFIC SITE:	Family Tree of Juan Carlos I
URL:	http://www.casareal.es/casareal/home.html

EXERCISES/ACTIVITIES

A. ¿Quiénes son? Interpretive Mode

Explique quiénes son los miembros de la Familia Real de España.

1. Juan Carlos I es _____ de Elena, Cristina y Felipe.

2. Sofía de Grecia es _____ de Juan Carlos I y _____ de Elena, Cristina y Felipe.

3. Elena y Cristina son _____ de Felipe.

4. Don Juan, Conde de Barcelona es _____ de Felipe.

5. Doña María de las Mercedes es _____ de Felipe.

6. Pilar y Margarita son _____ de Felipe.

7. Don Jaime Marichalar es _____ de Elena y _____ de Cristina.

> VARIATION 1: Have students write in the names of the family members instead of the relationship.
>
> 1. _____ es el padre de Elena, Cristina y Felipe.
>
> 2. _____ son las hermanas de Felipe.
>
> 3. _____ es el esposo de Elena.
>
> VARIATION 2: Focus mainly on Felipe, Príncipe de Asturias.
>
> 1. Felipe es _____ de Juan Carlos I y Sofía de Grecia.
>
> 2. Felipe es _____ de Elena y Cristina.
>
> 3. _____ son las tías de Felipe.

GENERIC WEB SITES:	Restaurants and menus
FOCUS:	Vocabulary: food, menu items
FUNCTION:	Ordering in a restaurant
CULTURE:	Mexican menu and typical food items
	Spanish menu and typical food items
SKILL:	Speaking
PROFICIENCY LEVEL:	Intermediate
STANDARDS:	1.1 Students engage in conversations, provide and obtain information, express feelings and emotions, and exchange opinions.
	1.2 Students understand and interpret written and spoken language on a variety of topics.
	2.1 Students demonstrate an understanding of the relationship between the practices and perspectives of the culture studied.
	2.2 Students demonstrate an understanding of the relationship between the products and perspectives of the culture studied.

4.2   Students demonstrate understanding of the concept of culture through comparisons of the cultures studied and their own.

SPECIFIC SITE: Menu for the restaurant Mediterraneo

URL: http://www.futurnet.es/arroceria/

EXERCISES/ACTIVITIES

A. *¿Qué tipo de restaurante es?* Interpretive Mode

¿Dónde se encuentra el restaurante Mediterráneo? Usando las fotos, describa el restaurante. ¿Cuál es su especialidad? Además de la comida, ¿qué otros servicios ofrece el restaurante?

B. *¿Cuáles son las categorías?* Interpretive Mode

Con un(a) companero(a) de clase, encuentren por lo menos tres platos que pertenecen a las siguientes categorías:

mariscos / pescados / vegetales / frutas / leche o crema

C. *En la Arrocería Mediterráneo.* Interpersonal Mode

Ud. y un(a) compañero(a) de clase están en Madrid y deciden comer en la Arrocería Mediterráneo. Pidan una entrada, un plato principal, un postre y una bebida. Otro(a) compañero(a) hace el papel del camarero(a).

D. *La cuenta.* Interpretive Mode

You decide to pay the bill with a credit card. You want to have an exact record of how much you spent in U.S. dollars so you can verify your credit card bill when it arrives at your home. Work with your partner and convert the prices for the various items you ate as well as the entire bill into U.S. dollars.

SPECIFIC SITE: Menu for El Papalote

URL: http://www.mex-mty.com/restaurantes/papalote/ papalote.html

EXERCISES/ACTIVITIES

A. *¿Qué tipo de restaurante es?* Interpretive Mode

¿Dónde se encuentra el restaurante El Papalote? Usando la información presentada, describa el restaurante. ¿Cuál es su especialidad?

B. ¿Cuáles son las categorías? Interpretive Mode

Con un(a) companero(a) de clase, encuentren por lo menos tres platos que pertenecen a las siguientes categorías:

carne / comida estadounidense / vegetales / leche o crema / frutas

C. En El Papalote. Interpersonal Mode

Ud. y un(a) compañero(a) de clase están en México, D.F. y deciden comer en El Papalote. Pidan una botana, un plato principal, un postre y una bebida. Otro(a) compañero(a) hace el papel del camarero(a).

The following activity is a good cross-cultural exercise that can be completed after completing the exercises for the menus for both restaurants above.

A. En Barcelona. Interpretive Mode

You and a friend arrived in Barcelona a few hours ago and you go to have your first meal in Spain. Your friend knows a little Spanish and without looking at the menu orders nachos, a chicken taco, and a burrito with frijoles on the side. The waiter looks very confused. Why is the waiter confused? What has your friend assumed about food in the Hispanic world? What would be some typical things to order in a Spanish restaurant?

GENERIC WEB SITES:	Schedules: Train schedules, movie schedules, TV schedules
	Listings: hotel listings, movie listings, restaurant listings
FOCUS:	Vocabulary: numbers, telling time, calendar terms
CULTURE:	Spanish transportation system, Spanish tourism industry, entertainment
SKILL:	Speaking
PROFICIENCY LEVEL:	Novice
STANDARDS:	1.1 Students engage in conversations, provide and obtain information, express feelings and emotions, and exchange opinions.
	1.2 Students understand and interpret written and spoken language on a variety of topics.
	2.1 Students demonstrate an understanding of the relationship between the practices and perspectives of the culture studied.

2.2   Students demonstrate an understanding of the relationship between the products and perspectives of the culture studied.

4.2   Students demonstrate understanding of the concept of culture through comparisons of the cultures studied and their own.

SPECIFIC SITE: Train Schedule for Madrid-Sevilla

URL: http://www.renfe.es

EXERCISES/ACTIVITIES

A. *Servicios y comodidades.* Interpretive Mode

¿Qué tren(-es) ofrece(-n) los siguientes servicios?

comida completa con servicio de camarero / comida ligera y bebidas / camas / literas / teléfono / bar

B. *¿Cuál es el mejor?* Interpretive Mode

Find a train for the following people.

1. el Sr. Morelos, un hombre de negocios que necesita estar en una reunión en Sevilla el viernes a la una y media

2. Carmen Robles, una estudiante universitaria que no tiene mucho dinero

3. la Sra. Suárez, una mujer muy rica que quiere viajar en una manera privada y lujosa; no le gusta levantarse temprano

4. una familia grande de padre, madre y cinco hijos que van a Sevilla el domingo para visitar a los abuelos; no tienen mucho dinero

5. dos turistas norteamericanos que no tienen mucho tiempo; quieren visitar el museo del Prado en Madrid por la mañana y el Alcázar de Sevilla por la tarde; no les importa el dinero

C. *Quisiera ir a Sevilla.* Interpersonal Mode

You go to the train station to purchase a ticket for Sevilla. Role-play the situation with a classmate who is the ticket agent.

SPECIFIC SITE: Hotel List for Madrid

URL: http://www.todoesp.es

EXERCISES/ACTIVITIES

A. *Servicios y comodidades.* Interpretive Mode

¿Qué hotel(-es) ofrece(-n) los siguientes servicios?

guardería / acceso minusválidos / piscina / golf / parking / céntrico

B. *¿Cuál es el mejor?* Interpretive Mode

Find a hotel for the following people.

1. una familia grande de padre, madre y cinco hijos que van a Madrid para visitar los museos

2. dos turistas norteamericanos que viajan en coche pero que quieren alojarse en el centro de Madrid

3. la Sra. Gaviria, una mujer muy rica que quiere viajar en una manera privada y lujosa

4. Roberto Alguilar, un estudiante universitario que no tiene mucho dinero

5. el Sr. Lado, un hombre de negocios que tiene muchas reuniones cerca de la Puerta del Sol

C. *Quisiera un buen hotel.* Interpersonal Mode

You and a friend/family member have just arrived in Madrid. Since your friend/family member doesn't speak Spanish, you must go to the tourist bureau to find a hotel room for the two of you. Role-play the situation with a classmate who is the agent in the tourist bureau.

Exercises and Activities for the Teaching of Grammar

Web site materials can also be used for the teaching and reinforcement of grammar structures. The following guidelines have been developed to aid in preparing exercises for the teaching of grammar.

- The visuals such as photographs and art work that accompany Web site texts can be used for a variety of exercises from simple description to narration to making conjectures.

- The Web site text can offer opportunities for identifying structural points and analyzing their use.

- The Web site can serve as a point of departure for additional exercises and activities to reinforce the grammar structure(s) being taught.

GENERIC WEB SITES: Descriptions of people

FOCUS: Grammar: adjective formation and placement

CULTURE: Description of peers in Hispanic culture

SKILL: Writing

PROFICIENCY LEVEL: Intermediate

STANDARDS: 1.2   Students understand and interpret written and spoken language on a variety of topics.

2.1   Students demonstrate an understanding of the relationship between the practices and perspectives of the culture studied.

2.2   Students demonstrate an understanding of the relationship between the products and perspectives of the culture studied.

4.1   Students demonstrate understanding of the nature of language through comparisons of the language studied and their own.

4.2   Students demonstrate understanding of the concept of culture through comparisons of the cultures studied and their own.

SPECIFIC SITE: Pepe's Personal Page
URL: http://www.uv.es/~pepem

EXERCISES/ACTIVITIES

A. *Describa a Pepe.* Interpretive Mode

Read the description of Pepe. Make a list of the adjectives that are used to describe him.

B. *Marta, la hermana de Pepe.* Presentational Mode

Marta is Pepe's twin sister. Prepare a description of Marta, using the description of Pepe as a model.

C. *Un autorretrato.* Describe yourself using the description of Pepe as a model but changing the information as necessary.

GENERIC WEB SITES: Current events from newspapers
FOCUS: Grammar: imperfect and preterite tenses
CULTURE: News about a variety of topics pertaining to Hispanic culture
SKILL: Writing
PROFICIENCY LEVEL: Intermediate High-Advanced
STANDARDS: 1.2   Students understand and interpret written and spoken language on a variety of topics.

2.1   Students demonstrate an understanding of the relationship between the practices and perspectives of the culture studied.

2.2   Students demonstrate an understanding of the relationship between the products and perspectives of the culture studied.

4.1   Students demonstrate understanding of the nature of language through comparisons of the language studied and their own.

4.2   Students demonstrate understanding of the concept of culture through comparisons of the cultures studied and their own.

SPECIFIC SITE: Spanish Daily Newspaper

URL: http://www.abc.es Http://www.elpais.es

EXERCISES/ACTIVITIES

A. *Las noticias*. Interpretive Mode

Students read a current news article chosen by the instructor. Students should make a list of the verbs in the imperfect tense and those in the preterite. Students should analyze why the particular tense is used.

B. *Un resúmen*. Presentational Mode

Students should write a brief summary of the news article paying particular attention to the use of the imperfect and preterite.

C. *Un(a) reportero(a)*. Presentational Mode

You are a journalist for the Hispanic edition of your local newspaper. Write a brief article about a recent event of local interest.

VARIATION 1: Locate a newspaper article that discusses an up-coming event. Change Exercises A, B, and C to a focus on the future tense and/or the *ir a + infinitive* construction.

Activities for Using the WWW for Research

According to Sinclair (1997) students can develop their critical thinking skills by learning to do research on the Web; by evaluating Web sites for authenticity and usefulness they can become discriminating information gatherers. Higgins (1996) also suggests that the WWW can be used for research projects in foreign language instruction.

The WWW is an excellent source of materials for research in the target language. Basic research activities involving the World Wide Web can be done at all language proficiency levels but are most effective when done with students who are at the intermediate level or higher. In general, the research activities involve the reading skill linked to the presentational mode of the speaking or writing skill. In order for students to complete the following suggested research activities, they will need to conduct research using a browser such as Netscape. As a result, no URLs are here provided.

A. *Un viaje ideal.* Presentational Mode

Divide the class into groups of five students each. Assign each student to role-play one of the members of a family of five that plans to take a trip to a Spanish-speaking country. Create a description of each family member outlining their interests using the following as a model:

Father:	Interested in photography, golf, and bird watching
Mother:	Interested in modern art and gourmet cooking
Fifteen-year-old boy:	Interested in music, soccer, and amusement parks
Five-year-old girl:	Interested in collecting dolls and swimming
Ten-year-old girl:	Interested in animals and ecology

The students are told how many days of vacation "their family" has and are given a certain amount of money to spend. Students must use Web site materials to research various aspects of the trip. They must decide which country/countries to visit and which cities within the country to visit. They must research hotels or other lodging and select the hotels/lodging where they will stay. They must pick restaurants. They must choose vacation activities that satisfy the interests of the various family members. The final product of the research will be a written itinerary of the planned trip. Students could also present their travel plans to the class in an oral presentation. Students should complete the research activity in three to four weeks.

B. *Nuestro mundo.* Presentational Mode

The environment and ecology are topics that are touched upon in most intermediate textbooks; they are also topics that are interesting to most students. There are various ways to formulate research activities based on this topic.

- Divide the broad topic into subtopics and assign each to an individual or pair. Topics could include recycling, endangered species, water pollution, air pollution, depletion of natural resources.

- Students could be expected to use their research to create posters, cross/teach to a lower level language class, create a multimedia presentation, create a video, write an article for a newspaper.

C. *Las noticias.* Students could research a topic of particular interest to one of the countries of the Spanish-speaking world. They could trace that topic over time by following the newspapers.

D. *La empresa multinacional.* Assign students to groups of four, all of whom are employees in a multinational firm. Assign each group to a Spanish-speaking country. The multinational firm is planning to open a branch in each of these countries. Have students research the country including its political stability, the demographics, the currency, its natural resources, its systems of communication and transportation in order to decide if it is feasible and economically sound to open a branch of the company in the country in question.

Conclusion

The preceding exercises and activities are meant to serve as generic models for the development of other exercises and activities that are linked to similar types of Web sites. It is hoped that with these suggestions instructors will be more willing to incorporate the World Wide Web into lesson plans. By using Web sites as a regular part of the classroom routine, students gain valuable insights into the target culture and language while simultaneously improving their lexical and grammatical accuracy and developing their reading, speaking, and writing skills. While the Web site exercises and activities focus on all five *Standards for Foreign Language Learning,* their continued use should help students "show evidence of becoming lifelong learners by using the language for personal enjoyment and enrichment" (Standard 5.2).

Notes

1. Since there are currently few Web sites that provide audio as well as visual information, exercises for developing the listening skill will not be treated in this article.
2. Interpersonal communication is direct communication between individuals who are in direct personal contact; it is characterized by active negotiation of meaning among individuals. The interpretive mode focuses on the appropriate cultural interpretation of meanings that occur in written or spoken form; it is one-way communication. The presentational mode refers to the creation of oral or written messages for an audience with whom there is no immediate personal contact. For a complete discussion of the three communicative modes see *Standards for Foreign Language Learning: Preparing for the 21st Century,* pp. 32-34.
3. For further information on the use of advance organizers see Spinelli & Siskin (1987).

4. For additional language learning activities based on the Internet, see Moehle-Vieregge's *Surf's Up!: A Website Workbook for Basic French/German/Spanish*. These three workbooks also provide hundreds of Web site addresses for current cultural information.
5. For further information on the role of vocabulary in communicative approaches to foreign language teaching see Spinelli & Siskin (1992).

References

ABC. [Online] Available http://www.abc.es.

Abrate, Jayne. 1997. "Using the World Wide Web to Teach Culture: Making the World a Smaller Place," pp. 150-162 in *Building Community Through Language Learning*, Robert Di Donato, ed. Selected papers from the 1997 Central States Conference on the Teaching of Foreign Languages. Lincolnwood, IL: National Textbook.

"Arbol genealógico de los ascendientes de la Familia Real Española." [Online] Available http://www.casareal.es/casareal/home.html.

"Arrocería Mediterráneo: La Carta." [Online] Available http://www.futurnet.es/arroceria/.

"Búsqueda de Alojamiento: Madrid." [Online] Available http://www.todoesp/es.

Fidelman, Carolyn G. 1996. "A Language Professional's Guide to the World Wide Web." *CALICO Journal* 13,2 and 3: 113-140.

Finnemann, Michael D. 1996. "The World Wide Web and Foreign Language Teaching," *ERIC/CLL News Bulletin* 20,1: 1, 6-8.

Galloway, Vicki. 1992. "Toward a Cultural Reading of Authentic Texts," pp. 87-121 in *Languages for a Multicultural World in Transition,* Heidi Byrnes, ed., Northeast Conference on the Teaching of Foreign Languages. Lincolnwood, IL: National Textbook.

García, Carmen. 1991. "Using Authentic Texts to Discover Underlying Sociocultural Information." *Foreign Language Annals* 24,6: 515-526.

Higgins, Chris. 1996. "The WWW for Instruction: Three Types of Activities and Projects." *IALL Journal of Language Learning Technologies* 29,1: 71-76.

"Horarios de RENFE: Trayectos." [Online] Available http://www.renfe.es.

Lafford, Peter A., and Lafford, Barbara A. 1997. "Learning Language and Culture with Internet Technologies," pp. 215-262 in *Technology-Enhanced Language Learning,* Michael D. Bush and Robert M. Terry, ed., ACTFL Foreign Language Education Series. Lincolnwood, IL: National Textbook.

Moehle-Vieregge, Linda, Lyman-Hager, Mary Ann, DuBravac, Stacy, Bradley, Travis, and Janis M. Yates. 1997. *Surfs Up!: A Website Workbook for Basic French*. Guilford, CT: Audio- Forum.

Moehle-Vieregge, Linda, Bird, Sabrina, and Manteghi, Christine. 1996. *Surfs Up!: A Website Workbook for Basic German*. Guilford, CT: Audio-Forum.

Moehle-Vieregge, Linda, Carbon, Lynn L., and James, Rodney A. 1997. *Surfs Up!: A Website Workbook for Basic Spanish*. Guilford, CT: Audio-Forum.

National Standards in Foreign Language Education Project. 1996. *Standards for Foreign Language Learning: Preparing for the 21st Century*. Lawrence, KS: Allen Press.

"Página personal de Pepe." [Online] Available http://www.uv.es/~pepem.

El País. [Online] Available http://www.elpais.es.

"El Papalote." [Online] Available http://www.mex-mty.com/restaurantes/papalote/papalote.html.

Rosenzweig, Steven M. 1996. "A W(orld) W(ide) W(eb) Starter Kit for Spanish Teachers," *Enlace: The Newsletter of the American Association of Teachers of Spanish and Portuguese* 10,2: 7-8.

Sinclair, Bryan T. 1997. "Teaching Students to Be Critical Thinkers on the Web," *The Teaching Professor* 11,3: 5.

Siskin, H. Jay, and Davis, Robert L. 1996. "Authentic Documents Revisited: Teaching for Cross-Cultural Understanding," pp. 1-18 in *Creating Opportunities for Excellence through Language*, Emily Spinelli, ed. Selected papers from the 1996 Central States Conference on the Teaching of Foreign Languages. Lincolnwood, IL: National Textbook.

Spinelli, Emily, and Siskin, H. Jay. 1987. "Activating the Reading Skill Through Advance Organizers. *The Canadian Modern Language Review* 44, 1: 120-133.

———. 1992. "Selecting, Presenting, and Practicing Vocabulary in a Culturally-Authentic Context. *Foreign Language Annals*. 25,4: 305-315.

"El tiempo." [Online] Available **http://www.abc.es.**

"El tiempo." [Online] Available **http://www.elpais.es.**

Walz, Joel. 1997. "The Internet as Textbook," pp. 139-149 in *Building Community Through Language Learning,* Robert Di Donato, ed. Selected papers from the 1997 Central States Conference on the Teaching of Foreign Languages. Lincolnwood, IL: National Textbook.

3
Toward the Creation of Virtual Classrooms
Electronic Mail and Cross-Cultural Understanding

Gerhard Fischer
Wisconsin Department of Public Instruction

The introduction of a new technology into the classroom forces us to think about its proper place within the larger framework of the purpose of foreign language education. Electronic mail is first and foremost a medium which allows us to communicate with others quickly and conveniently. It allows us to connect our students with their peers in other cultures. It also connects the teachers of these students. Such student and teacher communication through e-mail offers many opportunities for linguistic and cultural learning, and it focuses squarely on the over-arching purpose of foreign language learning as stated in the national *Standards for Foreign Language Learning* (National Standards 1996). These standards claim that "communication is at the heart of second language study" and that "it is the acquisition of the ability to communicate in meaningful and appropriate ways with users of other languages." In this paper I will offer some suggestions that may shed some light on what we may regard as meaningful and appropriate communication through e-mail. I will argue that this process of communication must be open-ended, student-centered and guided by the teachers. The metaphor of the "virtual classroom" will emerge from an interpretation of various examples of e-mail correspondence between students and teachers in German and American schools.

Cross-Cultural Communication and Community in Education

Whether or not we communicate person to person, whether or not we use paper and pencil, the telephone or electronic mail, all our communication

31

with speakers from another culture relies on similar techniques which allow us to reconstruct the context in which something is said. Claire Kramsch has demonstrated what unspoken assumptions underlie such communication and what it takes to negotiate the meanings of words which one usually takes at face value (Kramsch 1988, 1993a, 1993b, 1996). Such cross-cultural communication can be delightful and personally rewarding. It is without question also very hard work which requires the willingness to engage in the negotiation of the meanings of words and concepts as well as of personal relationships.

We know from our personal and professional lives that we enter conversations with certain goals in mind. In certain situations we may wish to provoke and irritate our partner, we may want to learn or to teach something, we may want to negotiate a deal, or we may simply engage in small talk—cognitively meaningless but socially important. In all these situations we are engaged in either the building or in the disruption of communities. I will assume throughout this paper that the purpose of foreign language teaching is not simply to facilitate communication, but more importantly the building of communities through communication. John Dewey (1916/1966) probably saw the link between communication and community most clearly. He emphasized the importance of thinking about the meanings of words in the daily process of negotiating the construction of our social realities. If we accept the fundamental importance of language in the process of building a community, the discussion of cross-cultural communication which involves at least two different languages becomes an issue of building a new community. This supports the sometimes fuzzy notion that we all need to become global citizens. The building of such communities should therefore become the primary focus in our foreign language classrooms.

E-mail and Cross-Cultural Communication

There are many reasons why teachers, perhaps foreign language teachers in particular, have become interested in using electronic mail in their classrooms. Whatever the reasons may be, e-mail communication has become an integral part of our lives. Doubtless e-mail is here to stay, and it will probably remain an important component in our daily correspondences no matter which direction the World Wide Web and other technologies are going. E-mail squarely focuses our attention on the written word and should therefore become an important tool in every classroom. As we have all experienced, it allows us to communicate in an instant with people all over the globe.

The challenge that is presented to all of us with the introduction of a new medium is that we have to explore what it can do and what it cannot do. Based on that understanding we can proceed to use it wisely as part of our overall classroom repertoire. In his analysis of the effects of television Neil Postman (1986), for example, points out that the television set could be used as a reading light. That, of course, is not what that medium was designed to do or how people use it daily. Likewise, one could use e-mail to design activities pattern drills and to teach grammatical rules. It is highly important for us to understand that this is not what this medium is normally used for. Again, e-mail makes it possible for us to communicate with other people quickly. One of the most striking characteristics of the daily use of e-mail is the brevity of messages and the expectation of almost immediate response. It is amazing how our notion of time has changed with the advance of new technologies. The telephone, the fax machine, cars, trains, and the jet aircraft have all changed our perception of time and space. Computer technology has changed the way in which we produce printed documents. The advancement of faster computers makes us laugh at the "dinosaurs" we used just five years ago. The few extra seconds it took those computers to respond to our commands are simply not acceptable any more. I am not saying that is good or bad. That's just the way it is. Time is of the essence in our use of e-mail, and we should take this into account when planning to use e-mail in our classrooms. We can then create a new space for a transatlantic learning community, a virtual classroom.

I am assuming throughout that the main purpose of the teaching of foreign languages is the creation of new communities, in which learners use language to construct or reconstruct each others' social realities (Searle 1995).

Readers with a deeper interest in the linguistic, anthropological and philosophical foundations of this discussion are reminded of the work by Mark Johnson and George Lakoff (1980), Lakoff (1996), Stephen Tyler (1978), John Searle (1995), Denzin and Lincoln (1994), or of Robert Bellah, Madsen, Sullivan, Swidler, and Tipton (1991). The broader discussion reflected in that work challenges formalist-objectivist assumptions that have dominated views which are at the foundation of language learning and teaching. In theoretical linguistics that school of thought is best expressed in the work of Zelig Harris (1951), Charles Fries (1945/1980), or Noam Chomsky (1957,1965). It is important to realize that the same school of thought has —over time—also created an educational environment which sees learning as a pure technicality and as the sequencing of carefully designed and controlled classroom activities whose outcomes can easily be measured. Herbert Kliebard's discussion of the "American Curriculum" (1995) provides many insights into the nature of this debate, from which John Dewey did not emerge as a highly influential force. Yet it is Dewey's work which pulls together the notions of community, communication, and general characteristics of learning. It is these notions which best support current views of the importance of communication and culture as expressed in the national standards.

Most of us likely do not want to be involved too deeply in these more theoretical discussion when it comes to the design of classroom practices and the use of new technology. But if we want to avoid the skepticism which is often derived from the perception that new developments in teaching are mere bandwagons (Grittner 1990) we need to understand that choices of instructional practices are linked to theoretical assumptions. Whether or not the availability of new technologies really complements the efforts of students to learn a new language depends to a large extent on how they are put to use (Donath 1994 and 1995a; Schwartz 1995). The decisions that each teacher faces daily, the decision of which instructional practice to use with the aid of which tools—paper and pencil, computer, television, blackboard etc.—is ideally rooted in the kind of discussion referred to above.

The Said and the Unsaid

Human communication involves complex systems of interaction. What is not said in conversations is often more important than what is said. Many examples have been given over the years of how various parts in our daily dealings with each other do not enter our consciousness. Friction, disharmony and the disruption of our lives are often the consequence (Tannen 1990; Watzlawick, Beavin, and Jackson 1967; Schulz von Thun 1982; Searle 1969; Austin 1962). Whether or not we follow speech and behavioral patterns that are idiosyncratic to specific cultures (German and American, for example) or subcultures (male and female, for example), one of the main challenges is to make us aware of the factors that influence what we say and how we say it. Once we are aware of these factors, we can bring that knowledge into our conversations with various partners and establish an engaging and meaningful learning community. In e-mail communication—as in all written communication—we must be very careful to say (write) what we mean to say. We cannot leave much unsaid. Leaving things unsaid (unwritten) brings with it the danger of misunderstandings, misinterpretation, and the failure to establish a community through communication. This is a dilemma not altogether different from the interpretation of literature or other texts which were written without the possibility of direct dialog in mind. In all these cases we reconstruct historical and cultural contexts. An interpretation of Goethe's or Shakespeare's plays, for example, must rely on our knowledge of the society and culture that they lived in. The reconstruction of the social reality of our e-mail partners is different and perhaps easier, because we can ask question when misunderstandings prevail. We can discuss what has been a misunderstanding or a difference in opinion in our respective classrooms, and if we want to take the process of understanding and communication further, we must express our thoughts openly and cannot simply treat messages as texts. We cannot leave our analyses unsaid, unless we care more about text analysis than about the process of cross-cultural understanding and the creation of communities.

One characteristic of e-mail communication, therefore, is its potential for the creation of learning communities through the written word in a space that is opened up by the speed of this medium. This is what sets it apart from the many other ways in which we learn about other cultures. There is still very little research on the properties of e-mail in the foreign language classroom. Accounts to date hardly pay attention to the development of a guiding metaphor like the virtual classroom, even though some excellent practical examples have been described in the literature (for example Abrate 1994, 1995; Trenchs 1996; Donath 1993, 1994, 1995b, 1997; Donath and Volkmer 1997). Yet the development of this metaphor may lead us to new possibilities in cross-cultural learning.

Legutke (1996, p. 15) captures the concept of the language classroom as "observatories from which both teachers and learners explore aspects of the target culture." He adds that it is evident that "the physical confines of the classroom are changed and thus substantially expanded: walls become display areas and are, at the same time, opened up to include the school library, the media center and the computer lab, but also the community beyond the school yard, and even communities in the target cultures." With e-mail, we can go one step further: We can add the dimension of the virtual classroom in which students learn about each other. These virtual classrooms are governed by similar rules as traditional classrooms. Students and teachers establish personal relationships, there is content that needs to be learned, teachers confer and complain about students much as in their staff room or faculty lounge at home, and there are discipline problems that need to be addressed.

E-mail projects conducted over a two-year period between two Wisconsin schools in the North Woods with schools in Lower Saxony and in Hessen as well as a quasi-ethnographic study of a high school in the Midwest with a school in the Hessian Rhein-Main area serve as the basis of insights regarding potential benefits of e-mail integration in the foreign language classroom. The teachers forwarded all e-mail messages to me that were exchanged by their students and between themselves. I did not know the students personally, but stayed in close touch with the teachers. My other insights come from my somewhat ethnographic study of Midwest High whose teacher and students had an e-mail connection with a school in the Hessian Rhein-Main area in Germany. I went to Midwest High[1] frequently to talk with students and teachers about their e-mail experiences. Most importantly, I persuaded the students to embark on a project that I hoped would bring out the best of possibilities in e-mail communication. I had to learn that this was not to happen.

Content and Relationships in E-mail Communication

The project idea that I brought to Midwest High was simple, and the German IV students and their teacher, Mary, were quite willing to try it out. Walter and his Hessian 12th grade students agreed to cooperate.

The idea called for the German and American students to watch the same movie and then to begin a transatlantic conversation about it. The conversation could be a critique of the movie, a review, or simply an exchange of opinions. Furthermore, the dialogue was supposed to be between the two classrooms and not between individual students but would adhere to the following pattern: Midwest High would watch the film, discuss it in class and form an opinion, very much like film critics would approach the discussion of a new movie. It would not matter in which language, English or German, the discussion would be carried out. The next step would be to write one fairly brief paragraph summarizing the group's discussion—now in German—and then to send this German summary to Hessen. Walter's class would respond in a similar fashion: They would read Midwest High's critique, discuss it in class and respond. This way, I hoped, a group conversation would get started that would have several advantages: First, Mary's group would not be intimidated from the beginning by having to formulate a critique in German. They would write the German paragraph as a group and would e-mail it to Midwest High. Second, knowledge would be constructed initially within each group of students, before the responses would be a challenge to negotiate meanings and opinions in the new virtual German-American classroom. Third, there would be a very strong focus on the content of messages as well as on the language in which it would be expressed: Students and teachers would work together to make the project a true cultural and linguistic learning experience. Fourth, this kind of project would move away from the uncommitted chat that can usually be observed in pen pal relationships.

To my knowledge, such a classroom-to-classroom dialogue and learning progression through e-mail has not been described anywhere in the literature.[2] The following comments will show that it did not work the way in which Mary and I had first envisioned it. The reasons why it did not develop as planned are interesting, however, and give many clues as to what some of the challenges of strong e-mail projects are.

The students agreed to watch the movie *Dead Poets' Society,* which was readily available in English in Germany and in German at Midwest. Beyond and above this practical advantage the students were interested in the way in which school curriculum and student-teacher relationships were portrayed in the film. Of course, the Midwest students did not learn anything about German culture through this movie. The German students may have gained some insights into the culture of U.S. boarding schools, but mostly the topics at hand provided a point of departure for the students in both countries to express how they feel about their schools and teachers. The purpose of showing a movie in this situation is therefore not to educate one group about the culture of the other. But it is suggested that all students would learn a great deal about both cultures in their discussions of the film. Such knowledge is constructed in their discourse.

Just before the Midwest students watched the film I decided that it might be helpful for the beginning of their critiquing conversation with the Germans to learn some useful expression. Even though the students had known me for quite some time by then, they were shy and reserved during that period. My plan was for the students to mention a film that they had seen recently and tell me what the title was, who the main actors were, whether it was a comedy, a mystery, an action-movie. Also, I wanted to know what the film was about, a very brief summary of the plot, and some personal observations. First we tried to talk in the whole group; then the students split up into small groups and worked on comments in German. I felt drained after the period. I had expected to get a lot more done, and based on what I had seen in other periods taught by Mary, I thought the students could do a lot more. One of the problems might have been that the students are not used to analyzing movies or literature this way. At least this is what Mary suspects. Therefore, the problem might not only have been that the students did not know the German words, but that they were unfamiliar with the kind of discussion I wanted them to have. Actually, in a later discussion they came up with far better ideas than the ones I had envisioned.

The beginning of the project therefore deviated from my plan, and subsequently many good ideas were not realized because strict timelines for the exchange of messages were not observed for a variety of reasons that I cannot detail here. One clear challenge was presented by the lengthy messages that were often sent by the Hessian students. When they sent a ten-page document that summarized their work over the course of a few weeks, for example, Midwest students had to treat that as a text that needed to be analyzed and interpreted in quite a few lessons. This task quickly turned into the kind of work that students are accustomed to from their textbooks and readers. Even though the information provided was valuable and personalized, this was not what we had had in mind for the e-mail project.

About a week after the Midwest students had watched the first half of *Dead Poets' Society* in German, we began to talk about the topics that might be interesting in a discussion with the Hessians. They had come up with a list of topics in German that could only be understood if explained by them, and they were more or less a shorthand for what they actually wanted to say. When a topic read, for example, "Prep Schools," this did not make sense to me. Also, what do students mean by "Private Schools (rules, agree/disagree?)" or "rich upper-class students?" After some initial clarification, students worked in groups to come up with topic formulations and questions in German. Mary and I walked around the classroom and helped out with vocabulary and grammar. The following is an example of what one group suggested as a message that would be sent to the Germans:

Fragen zum Thema: Private Schule/Oeffentliche Schule:

Wer soll für öeffentliche (public) Schulen und private Schulen bezahlen?

Was muss man machen, wenn er/sie Lust hat zu einer privaten Schule zu gehen?

Wann wäre eine Privat-Schule besser als eine public (öffentliche) Schule?

Sollten Leute die Steuern fuer Privatschulen bezahlen? etc.[3]

The movie which showed life in a private school gave the Midwest students the opportunity to talk about something that they were genuinely interested in. I was told that the subject of private school choice in Wisconsin was frequently talked about in the students' homes. This was therefore a topic much closer to their experience than I had assumed. The difficulty, however, was that private schools play a much less significant role in Germany. I feared that we would not get many responses from the German students, but the students wanted to send the messages anyway.

The response from Hessen was not surprising. The teacher—why not the students?—wrote that "private schools play a very insignificant role." He mentioned Montessori and Steiner schools and "boarding schools for well-to-do-parents, whose kids have problems in the regular schools."

Tucked away in the ten-page mailing that Midwest received from Hessen that day were six sets of interesting questions such as the following:

1. Frage: Die Schule im Film hat ein Motto. Unsere Schule hat keins, falls Eure Schule ein Motto hat, wie lautet es oder, wenn Ihr Eurer Schule ein Motto geben könntet, wie würde es lauten?

2. Frage (zum Lehrer-Schueler-Verhaeltnis): Ist Euer Verhältnis zu den Lehrern eher kühl-distanziert, freundlich, oder kameradschaftlich? Gibt es ähnliche Lehrer wie Keating auch bei Euch?

3. Frage: Wie läuft bei Euch allgemein der Unterricht ab? Sind es eher Vorträge, die Ihr zum Teil langweilig findet? Gibt es öfter so etwas wie Gruppen- oder Partnerarbeit? etc.[4]

What had happened in the process was that both groups of students, the Germans and the Americans, had used a similar format: They worked in groups and started asking questions that came out of their viewing of the film. This is an ideal opportunity, because the students are in charge within a learning situation designed by the teachers. One problem in this particular exchange was that the Midwest students had to spend much classroom time analyzing the lengthy texts that they received from Hessen. In general, there was no regular flow of e-mail between the two classrooms that would have enabled the cognitive learning process that I had first envisioned.

Much to my surprise, however, the students managed to establish personal relationships with their German partners. After struggling with German paragraphs and translations for a while, the Midwest students felt they wanted to communicate on a more personal basis with their Hessian partners—in English. "What will they think of us if we keep writing in baby-German?" one of them said. "Just let us write to them in English for a while." Apparently their teacher and I had overlooked the students' desire to establish personal relationships with the Germans and insisted too much on the discussion of content. Even though they "only" communicated through e-mail and did not even know their partners personally, they cared about the impression they might leave on them. So one day we just had the students write anything they wanted. The following are two examples:

> Liebe Nadine,
>
> I thought I could tell you about some of our high school sports. I am on the varsity team. We recently completed our four and a half month season. Our team only lost two games heading into the state tournament.
>
> We recently received your e-mail letters. One of our school policies is a responsibility pass. This pass is given to those students who are juniors or seniors who have good enough grades. It allows the student to leave school for one hour of the day. We are the only school in the state who allows students to do this. Our class will write further on this subject.
>
> I hope to hear from you soon.
>
> Erica

Erica shows pride in her athletic accomplishments, and perhaps she needs to tell her German key pals about this to gain some respect in their eyes. The second part of the message is related to the project. The Hessian students—prompted by the movie—had asked about rules and regulations at Midwest High. Erica responds to this but also refers to a larger response still to be developed by her class. The second example, a co-production by Connie and Lorie, is very similar:

> Hi! How are you? All our spring sports have started for the season. I (Connie) am in Track and Field, I (Lorie) am in no sports, but I am busy doing scholarship forms like many other seniors. How is school going for you?
>
> Did you enjoy Dead Poets' Society? We like the movie because it was realistically acted to get people to think abut the implications within their school and our society. We also think that the setting for the movie was an interesting insight into the world of the students in private schools compared to public schools. In response to some of your questions, the Midwest High School does not have a motto like

the school in the movie, but every year the Senior class comes up with a motto for the year they graduate . . . Another topic you brought up was the relationship between students and teachers. In reference to Keating, we have teachers who have some aspects of his methods of teaching—Frau Miller [Mary] is a good example—but some teachers are more traditional in their teaching methods. . . . In my opinion, if there's more openness in classes, more learning happens. The teachers who lecture to us all class generally aren't listened to as much. . . . I believe it is more interesting to discuss different subjects and share opinions with others.

Gotta go. Tschuss.

Connie and Lorie

Both messages are rich in cultural information. They also demonstrate that the students are perfectly able to discuss the movie pretty much the way I had envisioned it at the beginning. Perhaps they felt they could not do it in German, or they might not have been ready to do so when I wanted them to. Note that every message with content like this enables students and teachers to open up different cultural explorations. The students could go on to explore issues such as school discipline and regulations, the importance of athletic programs at American high schools and the complete lack of such programs in German schools, different teaching styles, and much more. We can leave the students the freedom to discuss what they are interested in, and teachers do not need to control the specific content that is addressed. It is important, however, that students are guided in their learning process. Teachers will have to encourage their students to ask questions and to give more detailed descriptions of their way of life. That will develop an understanding of cultural differences.

Their native English was the preferred language in which the students felt they wanted to define their relationships with the German partners. For the purposes of a German language class we need to insist that some German must be used. On another day we insisted on the use of German in a similar person-to-person communication situation. The most interesting observation on that day was that the Midwest students kept asking their teacher and me for help with their grammar. They cared what their peers thought of their German and wanted to write as accurately as they could. We—their teachers—merely acted as consultants, but we did not control or dictate what the students wrote. These are two examples:

Lieber Juergen,

Wie geht's? Uns geht es gut, aber wir sind sehr beschäftigt mit unseren Jobs, Hausaufgaben und Graduation Vorbereitungen. Unsere Prom ist am Samstag (Es ist eine grosse Tanz für unsere Schule. Wir tragen förmliche Kleidung da.)... Freitag und Samstag haben wir ein Schauspiel aufgeführt. Es war eine Komödie über uns und unseren Deutschunterricht. Es war sehr lustig, und wir hatten viel Spass....

Hallo alle—

Entschuldigung, meine Partnerin Rosie ist nicht in der Schule, und ich schreibe nicht so gut Deutsch, so ihr müsst mich dulden. Rosie ist heute zur Universität gegangen, aber das ist was sie hat unsere Lehrerin erzählt. Wirklich, sie ist jetzt zu Hause. Ich glaube, dass ich auch ein "Universität Besuch Tag" nehmen soll.

Hallo Melanie,

Ich habe am Montag deinen Brief gekriegt. . . . Danke für die photo. . . . Jetzt, ich will auf englisch schreiben, weil ich besser schreiben kann. . . . I was very impressed with all of the English that you wrote, and so when I write back I will write a lot in German. . . .[5]

The students are obviously perfectly capable of writing in German and expressing their thoughts in that language. Contacts outside the classroom were apparently established, contacts neither Mary nor I had been aware of. The letter to Melanie refers to letters and photos that had been exchanged. Perhaps in our original content-focused approach we had not thought enough about this part of the project. We overlooked that students need to form personal relationships. Sometimes one overlooks the obvious, and it is good that the students' contributions remind us of what can and what needs to be done.

Teacher Relationships

In all the projects that I have looked at so far, a large part of the communication occurred between the classroom teachers on either side of the Atlantic. This is necessary in order to establish agreement on the goals and of the organization of the project. What happens in the course of these planning sessions on the Internet, though, goes far beyond the exchange of information. The teachers strike up a personal relationship which is probably vital for the success of their project. We cannot deprive the students of the same opportunity if we want them to work successfully. During my analyses of e-mail projects, it became increasingly clear to me that we are in fact dealing with a learning experience in a newly created classroom. Even though the participants are far away from each other and rely on the written word only, the way in which learning in this community occurs resembles much of what we know from traditional classrooms.

Teachers, for example, talk about their students in the faculty lounge, in the hallways, or wherever they may meet. They also talk about things that are not related to school at all, and they take care of discipline problems in their classrooms. Some random examples are taken from my observation of the projects between the two schools in the Wisconsin Northwoods and their German partners.

Chit-Chat

The English teacher at the school in Lower Saxony, Liz, is a native of England. She and her partner from Wisconsin often talk about the weather, their own children, and of many other personal things. In November 1995, Liz writes:

> I do not know what the weather is like in Wisconsin just now but it has been very cold here in the past few days with temperatures dropping below freezing—much to my disgust. I do not know about you, but I dislike the cold intensely.
>
> Must stop now as our daughters should be in bed but I hear a lot of clattering going on so will have to sort them out.
>
> Do you actually come from Wisconsin since you mentioned your grandparents.
>
> All for now.
>
> Liz

Marge responds the next evening:

> Yes, the weather has been quite cold here, too. We just got two inches of snow and some sleet today . . . I will make sure all my students have written and match all their names for Monday. Nice to hear from you. I too need to get my daughter to bed. It's almost eight thirty.
>
> Marge

This is the kind of small talk that I had originally never provided room for in student projects. Yet—as adults— teachers need the building of this kind of community in order to be professionally successful. It seems to me that we cannot deny students the same opportunity.

Marge and Liz did an excellent job keeping the communication between their students going all year long. They did not focus on one particular project, but had their students write letters to one another which focused on traditional topics such as food, hobbies, and music. The students, just as their teachers, sent many personal notes. It was also evident that they exchanged letters and photos—as at Midwest High, this did not have to be encouraged by the teachers.

Classroom Discipline

When I observed the many messages that were exchanged in the Transatlantic Classroom (Donath and Volkmer 1997) in the discussion group "Teenage Life," my impression was that there was no teacher guidance or supervision over what the students wrote. Some contributions were frankly not appropriate for this kind of endeavor and probably did not contribute to any learning. One of the solutions in the TAC was to have moderators supervise and guide the discussions that occurred (Fischer 1998). This was one attempt to ensure that there was guided communication, but it may be hard for moderators who don't know the students and who do not have insight into the composition of the two learning groups to play the role of teacher. I suggest that it is necessary for any teacher to know the personalities of their students and the purpose of the cross-cultural contact in their own school curriculum.

In addition to this, some rules have to be imposed in order to facilitate discourse. In traditional classrooms, there are clear directions which tell students and teachers when everyone is allowed to talk or when personal comments are invited. No classroom can do without some rules. On the Internet, it must be clear that the classroom teachers in the participating traditional classrooms are still responsible for rules of conduct. They cannot abdicate their responsibilities to the more abstract and larger community, and they must know at all times what their students are doing and what kinds of messages they are posting. Messages such as the following were posted in the TAC over long periods of time and apparently went unnoticed by the teachers:

> Hello sweet boy's! We're two girls from Hamburg and we want to come to know YOU!!! We're 16 years old. We're looking for two boys which wanted to come to know us. S. has blond hair and blue eyes and I've got brown hair and brown eyes. Please write about a interesting theme. For example you and sex.

Such messages can usually be traced back to a minority of participating schools . They demonstrate that supervision cannot necessarily be taken for granted and that there is not necessarily a shared purpose that all participants have for the use of e-mail. This does not mean that such messages are never posted in a more supervised environment. The question is how they are dealt with. Consider the following exchange between Lake High in Wisconsin and a student in Hesse:

> Hi, ho you can call me Daniel,
> I live in W. . . . All what I do is Skaten, smoke weed and party's. I have a friend (from Australia) he live here for one year. . . . In my holidays I was in France, their were nice chik's and nice wave's, i heared in Australia are good wave's for surfing (but many shark's).
> I hope you write back fast.
>
> Daniel

Since this message was posted in an otherwise tightly controlled educational environment, there was immediate reaction by the teachers. The Wisconsin teacher writes her colleague:

> Lieber Bernhard:
>
> Der Brief 19 von D., kann ich im Klassenzimmer nicht lesen oder ausgeben. Der hat von "Weed" rauchen gesprochen, und ein paar andere Wörter benutzt... Die Schüler hier sprechen manchmal genauso, aber im Klassenzimmer geht das nicht. Bitte dem D. das erklären. Der Brief war an niemand und deswegen ist es kein Problem dass ich ihn rausschmeissen muss.
>
> Tschüss, Connie

Bernhard responds immediately:

> Dear Connie: Der Brief für M. war der "dubiose" Brief von Daniel. Ich werde am Mittwoch mit D. ein nettes Gespräch unter vier Augen führen und ich bin sicher, er wird freiwillig einen neuen Brief schreiben (sofern er nicht zufaellig krank ist). Ansonsten hat er in Kürze ein Problem mit meinen Arbeitsauftraegen, Noten usw....[6]

The way in which these students are supervised reminds me of small-town or village communities where everyone knows everyone's whereabouts and where people keep an eye on each other. This is possible on the Internet, and I believe it is necessary.

Conclusion

Most aspects of communication on the Internet that I have observed are not radically different from communication in a traditional classroom. In the traditional classroom teachers have to decide on content, on how they want to guide their students in their exploration of specific subject areas, and they have to foster a beneficial classroom climate. The challenge that is given to us by the medium of e-mail is mainly that this new community is based in two distinctly different cultures and that it deals with two different languages. Therefore, more attention than in the traditional classroom needs to be paid to contextualization and to the very conscious deliberation of what our partners in communication actually mean with the words that they use. Students and teachers have to make a very conscious effort to bring hidden assumptions about content and relationships to the forefront and to leave as little as possible unsaid. This learning process is no different from what we would encounter in student exchange situations when we have all students in the same school building. The beauty of e-mail is that this learning situation can be facilitated without travel. This means that many more students can benefit or that the student exchange experience can be enriched and prolonged.

One suggestion for the use of native and foreign languages in e-mail communication may provide the concluding comment. The plan to involve entire classrooms in group-to-group dialog can provide a distinct advantage over individual student-to-student communication. If an entire group agrees on drafting one short paragraph, teachers and students can work on content and linguistic correctness together. The process of drafting the contribution is then a communal learning process with input from all and without the risk of exposure of poor language skills that some weaker students may fear. This type of group interaction would then focus entirely on content, while individual student-to-student communication in the language of the students' choice can foster the kinds of relationships that are necessary for this directed learning process. Thus we may find a creative and productive way around the lasting question of which language we should use in direct dialog with native speakers from other countries.

Notes

1. All school and personal names in this paper are aliases.
2. The *Intercultural Classroom Conections* (IECC, available at http:\\www.stolaf.edu) list a number of interesting requests for partners in e-mail projects. Invitations to join book club discussion groups, for example, point to interesting project ideas.
3. Transl.: Questions on the topic: Private /public schools: Who should pay for public and private schools? What do you have to do if you want to go to a private school? In which situation would a private school be better than a public school? Should people pay taxes for private schools? etc.
4. Transl.: 1st question: The school in the movie has a motto. Our school does not have a motto, but if yours does, what is it, or if you could create a motto for your school, what would it be?—2nd question (in reference to student-teacher relationships): Is your relationship with your teachers more or less cool or distant, friendly or one of friendship among equals? Do you have teachers like Keating?—3rd question: What are your lessons normally like? Do they mainly consist of lectures which you find somewhat boring? Is something like partner or group work common? etc.
5. Transl: Dear Juergen, How are you? We are fine, but we are very busy with our jobs, homework and preparations for graduation. Our prom is on Saturday (that is a big dance for our school. We wear formal clothes on that occasion.). . . . Last Friday and Saturday we performed in a play. It was a comedy about ourselves and our German classes. It was very funny, and we had a lot of fun. . . . - Hello all- Sorry, my partner Rosie is not at school, and I don't write such good German, so you have to put up with me. Rosie went to the university today, but that is what she told our teacher. Really, she is at home. I think I should also take a University Visit Day.—Hello Melanie, I received your letter on Monday. . . . Thank you for the photograph. . . . Now let me write in English, because I can write better [in English].
6. Transl.: Dear Bernhard: I cannot use letter no. 19 (I hope the letter is at school, I am at home) from D. in the classroom. He talked about smoking weed, and he used some other words.... The students here sometimes talk just like that, but that is impossible in the classroom. Please explain that to D. The letter was not addressed to anyone in particular, and so it does not create a problem that I have to throw it out. Bye, Connie.—Dear Connie: The letter for M. was the mysterious letter from D. I will have a nice talk with D. and I am sure he will volunteer to write a new letter (unless he happens to be out sick). Otherwise he will have a problem with my assignments, grades, etc. very soon.

References

Abrate, Jayne. 1994. "Authentic Communication via Minitel." In: Gale K. Crouse, ed., *Meeting New Challenges in the Foreign Language Classroom.* Report of the Central States Conference on the Teaching of Foreign Languages. Lincolnwood, IL: National Textbook Company.

————. 1995. Integrating Minitel and French Culture in the Classroom. In: Gale Crouse, ed., *Broadening the Frontiers of Foreign Language Education.* Report of the Central States Conference on the Teaching of Foreign Languages. Lincolnwood, IL: National Textbook Company.

Austin, J. L. 1962. *How To Do Things With Words.* Edited by J. O. Urmson. Oxford: Oxford University Press.

Bellah, Robert N., Madsen, Richard, Sullivan, William M., Swidler, Ann, and Tipton, Steven M. 1991. *The Good Society.* New York: Alfred A. Knopf.

Chomsky, Noam. 1957. *Syntactic Structures.* Ninth Printing. The Hague, Netherlands: Mouton (1971).

————. 1965. *Aspects of the Theory of Syntax.* Cambridge, MA: The M.I.T. Press. (Third paperback printing, October 1970.)

Denzin, Norman K., and Lincoln, Yvonna S. (eds.). 1994. *Handbook of Qualitative Research.* Thousand Oaks, CA: Sage Publications.

Dewey, John. 1916/1966. *Democracy and Education.* New York: The Free Press.

Donath, Reinhard. 1993. "Message Received from Bronx: Electronic Mail öffnet Klassenräume für interkulturelles Lernen." In: *Medien Praktisch 3/1993.* Germany.

————. 1994. "Opening the Classroom - Electronic mail im Englischunterricht." In: *RAAbits Englisch.* Heidelberg, Germany: Raabe-Verlag.

————. 1995a. "Schluß mit der Simulation im Englischunterricht! Mit electronic mail auf die Datenautobahn." In: *Computer und Unterricht 18/1995,* Germany.

———— 1995b. "Schreiben am Computer: Klassenkorrespondenz per electronic mail." In: Bernd Kast, ed., *Fertigkeit Schreiben. Fernstudienprojekt zur Fort-und Weiterbildung im Bereich Germanistik und Deutsch als Fremdsprache.* Muenchen, Germany: Langenscheidt Verlag.

————. 1997. *Internet und Englischunterricht.* Stuttgart, Germany: Klett-Verlag.

Donath, Reinhard, and Volkmer, Ingrid (eds.). 1997. *Das Transatlantische Klassenzimmer.* Hamburg, Germany: Körber-Stiftung.

Fischer, Gerhard. 1994. "The Semantics of Culture: Communication and Miscommunication in the Foreign Language Classroom. " In: Gale K. Crouse, ed., *Meeting New Challenges in the Foreign Language Classroom.* Report of the Central States Conference on the Teaching of Foreign Languages. Lincolnwood, IL: National Textbook Company.

————. 1998. *E-mail in Foreign Language Teaching—Toward the Creation of Virtual Classrooms.* Tübingen, Germany: Stauffenburg Verlag.

Fries, Charles C. 1945/1980. *Teaching & Learning English As A Foreign Language.* Ann Arbor: The University of Michigan Press.

Grittner, Frank. 1990. "Bandwagons Revisited: A Perspective on Movements in Foreign Language Education." In: Diane W. Birckbichler, ed., *New Perspectives and New Directions on Foreign Language Education.* Lincolnwood, IL: National Textbook Company.

Harris, Zelig S. 1951. *Structural Linguistics*. Chicago, IL: Phoenix Books. The University of Chicago Press (Eighth Impression, 1969).

Johnson, Mark, and Lakoff, George. 1980. *Metaphors We Live By*. Chicago, IL: The University of Chicago Press.

Kliebard, Herbert M. 1995. *The Struggle for the American Curriculum*. 1893-1958. Second Edition. New York: Routledge.

Kramsch, Claire. 1988. "The Cultural Discourse of Foreign Language Textbooks." In: Alan J. Singerman, ed., *Toward a New Integration of Language and Culture*. Middlebury, VT: Northeast Conference on the Teaching of Foreign Languages.

———. 1993. *Context and Culture in Language Teaching*. Oxford: Oxford University Press.

———. 1993a. "Language Study as Border Study: Experiencing Difference." In: *European Journal of Education*, Vol. 28, No. 3.

———. 1996. "Toward a Dialogic Analysis of Cross-Cultural Encounters." In: *Gießener Diskurse-Begegnung mit dem Fremden*. Gießen, Germany: Verlag der Ferber'schen Universitätsbuchhandlung.

Lakoff, George, 1996. *Moral Politics*. Chicago, IL: The University of Chicago Press.

Legutke, Michael. 1996a. "Redesigning the Language Classroom." In: Christ, H. and Michael Legutke (eds.). *Fremde Texte verstehen. Festschrift für Lothar Bredella*. Tübingen, Germany: Narr Verlag.

———. 1996b. "Begegnung mit Fremden - via e-mail?" In: Gießener Diskurse-Begegnung mit dem Fremden. Gießen, Germany: Verlag der Ferber'schen Universitätsbuchhandlung.

National Standards. 1996. *Standards for Foreign Language Learning: Preparing for the 21st Century*. National Standards in Foreign Language Education Project. Lawrence, KS: Allen Press, Inc.

Postman, Neil. 1986. *Amusing Ourselves to Death*. New York: Penguin Books.

Schulz von Thun, Friedemann. 1982. *Miteinander reden: Störungen und Klärungen. Psychologie der zwischenmenschlichen Kommunikation*. Reinbek bei Hamburg, Germany: Rowohlt Tachenbuch Verlag.

Schwartz, Michael. 1995. "Computers and the Language Laboratory: Learning from History." In: *Foreign Language Annals* 28, 4.

Searle, John R. 1969. *Speech Acts. An Essay in the Philosophy of Language*. Cambridge: Cambridge University Press.

———. 1995. *The Construction of Social Reality*. New York: The Free Press.

Spradley, James P. 1979. *The Ethnographic Interview*. New York: Harcourt Brace Jovanovich College Publishers.

Tannen, Deborah. 1990. *You Just Don't Understand. Women and Men in Conversation*. New York: Ballentine Books.

Trenchs, Mireia. 1996. *Writing Strategies in a Second Language: Three case studies of learners using electronic mail*. In: The Canadian Modern Language Review, Volume 52, No. 3.

Tyler, Stephen A. 1978. *The Said and the Unsaid. Mind, Meaning, and Culture*. New York: Academic Press.

Watzlawick, Paul, Beavin, Janet H., and Jackson, Don D. 1967. *Pragmatics of Human Communication. A Study of Interactional Patterns, Pathologies, and Paradoxes.* New York, NY: Norton & Company, Inc.

Wolcott, Harry F. 1990. *Writing Up Qualitative Research.* Qualitative Research Methods Series, Volume 20. Newbury Park, CA: Sage Publications.

———. 1994. *Transforming Qualitative Data.* Thousand Oaks, CA: Sage Publications.

Wolf-Manfre, Eva. 1996. "Das Transatlantische Klassenzimmer aus der amerikanischen Perspektive." In: *Bericht zur Konferenz "Online Projekte in den deutsch-amerikanischen Beziehungen."* Hamburg, Germany: Koerber Stiftung.

4
Teaching Strategic Competence to High School Spanish Students

Linda Paulus

Kathleen Hajek

José Felipe Acosta
Mundelein High School

Introduction

Most high school teachers recognize the desirability of using more of the target language (L2) in the classroom. Secondary teachers also know intuitively, if not from the research itself, that there is a direct correlation between quantity and quality of foreign language input that students are exposed to and the quantity and quality of their comprehension of the written and spoken L2. Yet many students experience limited exposure to the spoken L2 for a variety of reasons. For example, some teachers believe that beginning students would become "lost" if their teachers spoke to them exclusively in the L2. Often, students' exposure to the foreign language in their classes is quite limited. As a result, many students lack sufficient comprehension and production skills to interact comfortably with anyone other than the classroom teacher, and their communication is limited to previously studied topics. In addition, many high school students can't resist the temptation to push the teacher to speak English, and are accustomed to using English when they need to communicate with classmates and/or with their instructor.

Four years ago, Mundelein High School Spanish teachers made a collective decision to increase the use of the L2 in the classroom in order to provide their students with the maximum opportunity to acquire Spanish. Two important questions we faced were: (1) how to encourage the maximum use of comprehensible input in the classroom, i.e., how to approach immersion during classtime, and (2) how to establish when English was necessary. Because our goal was maximum competence in written and spoken Spanish, we understood the need to expose our students to as much Spanish as possible. Our first task was to define immersion. In the context of Spanish classes at Mundelein High School, immersion means that we teach students to depend on Spanish, rather than English, to process new information. Even beginning students learn vocabulary, grammar, and culture in Spanish. Students learn to use Spanish to approach new experiences and to learn new material. They understand that we avoid translation whenever possible when we communicate with each other, either in spoken or in written Spanish as we teach new material. We also help students learn to do the same. One challenge was to implement immersion in an admittedly artificial environment. After all, students are not truly immersed in the target language when announcements are in English and English is the primary language before and after class in the hallways and in other classes.

Despite the challenges posed by a high school setting, Mundelein teachers focused on ways to implement immersion in a foreign language classroom. Many previously overlooked opportunities for increasing students' exposure to comprehensible input are now being exploited by teachers and students alike. Immersion at Mundelein has come to mean that teachers look for every opportunity to provide students with comprehensible input in the target language as a means for teaching the vocabulary, grammar, and cultural program outcomes. English plays a small but important role early in the Spanish program, primarily as a vehicle for teaching students *strategies* for studying and surviving in an immersion setting. In a nutshell, Spanish language and cultures are taught entirely in the L2, whereas the metacognitive aspect of language acquisition, the learning *how* to learn Spanish, is taught early in the first year in English.

Setting the Stage for Immersion

Mundelein High School is a mid-sized secondary school northwest of Chicago, Illinois, and is on a 4 by 4 block schedule. Students who take Spanish are in class for 90 minutes per day, five days per week, and complete the traditional one year of Spanish in two terms of nine weeks each (the equivalent of one semester.)

Starting about five years ago, Mundelein made a commitment to revise the foreign language curricula so that they became more learner-centered and included measurable outcomes. Foreign language teachers in the International Studies Division wrote a First-Year Modern Language curriculum driven by its purpose statement:

The purpose of foreign language study at Mundelein High School is to comprehend the target language; to be able to communicate orally and in writing in that language; and to display an awareness of, a sensitivity toward, and an appreciation for cultural diversity.

In order to accomplish this task, Spanish teachers developed a curriculum that immersed students in Spanish. We recognized the need to help students survive for 50 (and now 90) minutes in a classroom for five days per week. We agreed with the research that immersing students in comprehensible input best prepares them to survive and thrive outside the classroom in a situation in which their conversational partners may be non-English speakers (Krashen and Terrell 1983; VanPatten 1986).

Once the performance-based curriculum was written, defining terms was necessary. For example, if total immersion is the ideal, what does immersion in the Spanish classroom look like and sound like in the beginning of Spanish I, when students have little or no comprehension of spoken Spanish? Currently, it looks like this: during the first weeks of class, immersion consists of extended periods of input in Spanish made comprehensible via use of TPR, visual aids, cognates, video, pair work on the basics such as numbers and the alphabet, dictations, games, competitions, and other input-rich activities. Throughout the first two weeks of the course, students take time out from Spanish for short (ten to twenty minutes) sessions in English to explore the nature of communication, language acquisition, and to learn about the techniques they and the teacher will use to accelerate their comprehension, reading, speaking, and writing performances in Spanish.

An important goal for our students is to be able to communicate their needs in case they are ever in a situation with a native speaker who does not speak English. Students learn that neither English nor silence is a viable option for sustaining communication in such a situation, so neither is considered a viable option in our classes. Since beginners have little or no L2 vocabulary, a primary focus for classroom activities throughout much of level one is to develop students' Strategic Competence .

Strategic Competence as a Performance Goal

Students learn that Strategic Competence is the ability to make the most of the language you do have to stay in the L2 no matter what. A student strong in Strategic Competence is comfortable with the language s/he has and is unfazed by a conversation instigated by someone other than the usual instructor, including those with native speakers. Strategic Competence kicks in, we tell the students, when speakers try to communicate on topics about which they have limited language capability due to missing vocabulary and/or cultural knowledge (Lee and VanPatten 1995: 149). Students who are strategically competent have strategies at their disposal to help manipulate the speech of the more advanced conversational partner, whether that partner is the teacher or any other Spanish speaker that they encounter. Such students utilize phrases such as: *Hable más despacio, por favor (Speak more slowly, please); Repita, por favor (Repeat, please); No comprendo (I don't understand); ¿Comprende? (Do you understand?)* to help make comprehensible any incomprehensible Spanish they hear. They often use defining and/or circumlocution phrases to help stay in Spanish: *una cebra es como un caballo, pero es blanco y negro. Vive en Africa. (A zebra is like a horse but it is black and white. It lives in Africa).* In addition, they utilize gestures to help get their point across. Finally, they demonstrate a lower level of nervousness when first encountering unfamiliar topics, speakers and/or language.

Teachers strongly encourage the development of Strategic Competence, especially, but not exclusively, in the beginning levels for two reasons. First, Strategic Competence enables students to deal with unfamiliar speakers on unfamiliar topics. Second, Strategic Competence development facilitates maximum use of the L2 both in the classroom and in student work at home. This focus has powerful implications for both teacher and student behavior in the classroom. It drives classroom conversation, vocabulary introduction and expansion, and testing.

Teacher as Catalyst for Strategic Competence

We have two major responsibilities at the beginning of our language program. First, we help students "buy in" to immersion when we explain the language acquisition process and how students can take advantage of their knowledge of the process in order to do well in class. We use Krashen's Input Hypothesis as an explanation for the necessity for maximum exposure to the L2 for acquisition to take place (Krashen and Terrell 1983). Students learn that input—the L2 they hear and read in and out of the classroom—is the engine that will drive their eventual speech production. Further, students must be able to depend on us to make that input comprehensible to them. That is, students must be able to understand key words and concepts of the input they read or hear, and communicate to us immediately if they lose the gist of the conversation.

The second major responsibility we have is to use every opportunity to speak Spanish in our interaction with students and to teach students how to avoid English as the language of communication in the classroom. The ability to provide a steady, sustained flow of comprehensible input, and to get students to attend to that input, are talents worth developing since we wish to see rapid production from our students. In order to provide comprehensible input, we exploit our students' background knowledge and use vocabulary and grammatical structures that are very to somewhat familiar to students.

However, comprehensible input also must contain just enough unfamiliar language so that students who attend to it can continue their L2 acquisition. The students' understanding of every single word in the L2 is neither desired or expected. Input that never contains unfamiliar vocabulary and grammar does not help the students to progress in their comprehension and speech development. Input that contains no familiar language and structures and very few or no contextual clues, becomes incomprehensible input and is of no help in the development of student speech. (Krashen and Terrell 1983 and elsewhere). Instead, an environment rich in incomprehensible input is analogous to turning on the radio and listening to a steady stream of talk radio in a foreign language. The likelihood that radio listeners would acquire the language they hear under these circumstances is almost nil.

Just as important as the teacher's ability to provide comprehensible input is the teacher's attitude toward English usage in the classroom. If a teacher often bows to pressure from students to resort to English when they don't understand a vocabulary item or a topic during a conversation, Strategic Competence will be weak or nonexistent for most of those students. The more teachers develop students' Strategic Competence, the more students' confidence and ability to stay in the L2 improve. The need for English diminishes accordingly.

Techniques for Developing Strategic Competence

We use three primary tools for teaching to Strategic Competence: (1) we provide visual linguistic support in input, in handouts and around the classroom for students to get their daily needs met in the L2; (2) we aim for highly comprehensible input built into daily lesson plans (our philosophy is the less translation, the better), and (3) students undergo formal benchmark testing twice per course, part of which entails being evaluated on the extent of their Strategic Competence.

Linguistic Support

First, we prepare beginning students to deal with the sustained flow of spoken Spanish that is about to come their way. Teachers teach and test a list of useful survival expressions (Figure 1) for students to memorize. (Presentation of this list is one of the very rare occasions when translation is employed to help students understand the L2). Complex grammatical structures are taught as lexical items, i.e., the phrases *Hable más despacio, por favor* and *¿Corrigió usted los exámenes? (Speak more slowly, please* and *Did you correct the exams?)* are not explained as examples of the formal command and the third person singular preterite forms of the verbs *hablar (to speak)* and *corregir (to correct)*. At this stage, students could care less about the grammar involved. What they need is a phrase that will get them immediate results, more comprehensible speech coming at them, and a grade they're curious about, respectively. It is vital, however, that the teacher not only teaches survival phrases, but uses them with the students. When teachers say *No comprendo, repita eso, por favor (I don't understand, repeat that please)* under logical circumstances, their students incorporate it in their speech in a natural way as well (Musumeci 1996).

Students also benefit from one or two early pep talks about cognates, and their utility in their comprehension. If teachers provide examples of the great quantity of cognates that exist between Spanish and English, and then look for every opportunity to incorporate cognates in input, students' comprehension will rise accordingly. For example, first year students who were asked the question *¿Quién ganó el partido? (Who won the game?)* knew *partido (game)*, and *quién (who)* but were stumped by *ganó. (won)*. The paraphrase: *¿Cuál fue el equipo superior? (Which was the superior team?)* resulted in many "aaaahhhs ... ah-ha! Yo comprendo...."

Finally, it is our experience that English usage goes down dramatically when students have easy access to phrases that help them get their needs met in class. Students find visual linguistic support posted on the walls in the form of "language ladders." Language ladders consist of strips of paper upon which high-frequency words and phrases are printed and grouped according to semantic fields. For example, English usage usally becomes more prevalent during game playing because beginning students often don't know how to say *Me toca a mí (It's my turn), Es tu turno,¡Ya! (It's your turn , Go!)* or *¡Estás haciendo trampa! (You're cheating!)* They get excited during the game and shout such phrases without thinking. Students will use these same phrases in Spanish during game playing if the teacher teaches and reviews them one by one over the course of several days and, most importantly, uses the phrases in class as well. Other examples of semantic fields include *Tengo que pedirte un favor (I have to ask you a favor)*: *¿Me puedes prestar un lápiz? (Can you lend me a pencil?) Dame una hoja de papel, por favor (Give me a sheet of paper, please); Estuve ausente; ¿puedo copiar tus apuntes? (I was absent; can I copy your notes?) La confusión: No entiendo (I don't understand); Repita eso, por favor (Repeat that, please); no puedo oír (I can't hear); no puedo ver (I can't see); Baje la lámina, por favor (Lower the transparency, please); El permiso (permission): ¿Me permite hablar en inglés? (May I speak in English?); ¿Me da permiso tomar agua? (May I get a drink of water?)*; and so on. Teachers decide the phrases that best meet the needs of their students under categories such as *Los saludos/Las despedidas/Las excusas (Greetings/leave-takings/excuses)* and introduce them gradually and steadily. One cautionary note: it is usually counterproductive to introduce many categories with many phrases in each category all at once. Instead, consider introducing one or two categories per day, and one or two phrases per day, depending upon the need and the complexity of the phrase. If phrases are introduced gradually and reviewed in context, there is no need to post the English translations.

One particularly important language ladder is *La Circunlocución*. Teachers facilitate students' ability to process information from Spanish to Spanish rather than from Spanish to English or vice versa by providing students with circumlocution phrases, by using them themselves, and by requiring that students use them in class and in homework. High-frequency classroom expressions include phrases such as *es una cosa/una persona/un lugar que... /es similar de/se usa para; es lo contrario/lo opuesto de... (it's a thing/a person/a place that... /it's similar to... /it's used for...; it's the opposite of...)* and so on. Teachers who model vocabulary presentation and explanation by using these phrases can count on similar production skills on the part of their students.

Daily Comprehensible Input

During the introduction of new vocabulary, teachers avoid translation as a means of conveying the meaning of new vocabulary. Instead, new vocabulary is introduced by defining it in Spanish via synonyms *(una chica es una muchacha) (A girl is a girl)*; cognates *(un profesor es un director de la clase) (A teacher is the director of the class)*; or explanations using circumlocution phrases *(Un lápiz se usa para escribir... es de color amarillo y es largo.) (A pencil is used to write . . . it's yellow and it's long)*. Teachers use visual aids such as drawings, photos from a picture file, overhead transparencies that accompany the text, gestures, mime, and realia when applicable. Conversations are woven around a visual cue or a highly familiar topic. One useful input activity for beginners during the first few days of school includes learning the names of students by associating their names with the clothing and colors they are wearing. A typical exchange begins with the teacher incorporating many cognates in the input, and with writing cognates on the board as they arise during the conversation, e.g., *los colores, rosado, la blusa (the colors, pink, the blouse)* and so on. Students deduce the meaning of non-cognates such as *la ropa* if the teacher sets up columns and provides a number of cognates *(la blusa, las sandalias, los pantalones, los shorts)* before pointing out and adding non-cognates *(la camiseta, el vestido) (the T-shirt, the dress)* to the list. Typical conversations designed to provide input begin with questions such as *¿Cuál es tu nombre? ¿Cómo te llamas? Me llamo _____ (What's your name? My name is ___)* and includes exchanges such as the following:

> *Estudiantes, silencio por favor. Escuchen muy bien* (cups ear to aid comprehension.) *Miren a esta persona aquí* (walks over to student and gestures to aid comprehension of *blusa*.) *Esta chica lleva una*

blusa blanca; el color es blanco (writes *blanco* on the board under the header, *los colores*). *Mi nombre es* _____.(points to self). *¿Cómo te llamas? (Ana). Ella se llama Ana. Ana lleva una blusa blanca.*

Students, quiet, please. Listen carefully (cups ear to aid comprehension.) *Look at this person here* (walks to student and gestures to blouse to aid comprehension of *blouse.*) *This girl is wearing a white blouse. The color is white* (writes *white* on the board under the header, *the colors*). *My name is* _____. *What's your name? (Ana). Her name is Ana. Ana is wearing a white blouse.*

The instructor goes on to introduce two or three other students at a time, weaving input around the students, their clothing, and/or objects that are easily associated with them *(la mochila verde, los lentes, la bolsa pequeña) (the green backpack, the glasses, the small purse).*

Students develop Strategic Competence when they experience regular classroom testing of listening comprehension as well as definition and circumlocution skills. Pop quizzes for listening comprehension are easy to administer and to grade. In a typical *dictado* in which students listen to a description of selected people in class, or of photos or drawings, teachers ask students to number a paper from one to five, and to write the name of the person, or the name of the object that corresponds to each description. A variation on this activity is to have students draw and color an illustration according to instructions from the teacher. Activities of this type provide students with the vocabulary and the confidence to explain in Spanish, rather than to rely on translation to get their meaning across.

Another technique we use to teach students to circumlocute is to create clusters, or *mapas semánticos* in Spanish. *Mapas semánticos* are a powerful tool for review of old and current vocabulary. They are a kind of snapshot of the quantity and quality of language stored in the students' memories. Students scan previous vocabulary lists to look for words they can associate with new vocabulary. Each main word is circled, and associated words are "clustered" in bubbles off the main words. Each bubbled word can suggest new associations (Lusser Rico 1983: 35-38). *Mapas semánticos* are not graded for spelling and grammatical errors; perfect Spanish is not the goal of this activity. Instead, the goal is to rapidly acquire enough vocabulary so that defining and describing in Spanish become easy for the student.

Once students learn the simple association techniques to make their maps for vocabulary practice, they are ready for homework assignments in which they define vocabulary. They are ready for tests as well. Tests of this type can take a number of forms. In one variation, the teacher writes the definitions and ask the students to write the corresponding words. In another, the student writes definitions to cues provided by the teacher. A third variation is to have students write the definitions and earn points only if the teacher can guess the word being described. Typical Spanish I definitions include explanations (along with grammatical errors) such as: *un batido es helado y leche fría es una bebida o postre (a milkshake is ice cream and cold milk it's a drink or dessert); un vegetariano es una persona que come solamente verduras (a vegetarian is a person who eats only vegetables); comilón es una persona que come mucho (a glutton is a person who eats a lot); jugo es el agua de fruta, una bebida de desayuno, por ejemplo, jugo de naranja (juice is the water of fruit, a breakfast drink, for example, orange juice.)*

The *Prueba relámpago (lightening quiz)* is *an oral counterpart to written tests and activities such as those described above.* The *Prueba relámpago* is a short, timed opportunity for students to earn test or participation points; students select words posted on an overhead or the board behind the instructor (or behind another student) for the listener to guess. Fifteen or so words are posted; students pick a word they want to define and jot it down. Then, for five to eight minutes or so, students earn points for every word they describe well enough for the teacher to guess. If the teacher can't guess, the speaker earns no point. Students are encouraged to help each other to provide greater details to aid guessing.

Pruebas relámpagos are a kind of "dipstick" to measure to what extent students are developing Strategic Competence in Spanish. They are a way around the artificial environment imposed by a classroom setting; in a real conversation with native speakers who are not bilingual, our students would be forced to define, describe, and circumlocute in Spanish if they were intent on meeting their needs because their vocabulary, by comparison, is limited. Teachers use *Pruebas relámpagos* frequently to create the need for and to measure their Strategic Competence. In addition, the nature of this type of quiz is such that students are assured of a number of opportunities to hear comprehensible input and to accumulate points for their own participation grade.

Even grammar can be taught in the L2. During week three of Spanish I, one instructor wished to introduce noun-adjective agreement. After debating whether to teach the grammar in English or in Spanish, she decided to exploit the cognates inherent in the topic and teach the grammar in Spanish. She began the input segment by writing the following on the board:

sustantivo   verbo   adjetivo   adverbio

TEACHER: ¿Comprenden ustedes estas palabras? (gestures)

STUDENTS: Tres sí; uno, no.

TEACHER: Explíquenme la palabra *verbo.*

STUDENT 1: A verb.

TEACHER: No comprendo.

STUDENT 2: ¿Acción?

TEACHER: Bueno. Y ¿un adjetivo?

STUDENT 3: ¿Describe en español?

TEACHER: Sí, describe. Y, ¿qué describe un adjetivo?

STUDENTS: ¿persona?

TEACHER: Sí, describe a personas, y ¿qué más?

STUDENTS: Objeto y lugar.

TEACHER: Entonces, ¿qué es un sustantivo?

STUDENT 4: Persona, lugar, cosa.

(Translation)

TEACHER: Do you understand these words? (gestures)

STUDENTS: Three, yes, one, no,

TEACHER: Explain the word *verbo.*

STUDENT 1: A verb.

TEACHER: I don't understand.

STUDENT 2: Action?

TEACHER: Good. And an adjective?

STUDENT 3: It describes in Spanish?

TEACHER: Yes, it describes. And what does it describe?

STUDENTS: Person?

TEACHER: Yes, it describes people, and what else?

STUDENTS: Object and place.

TEACHER: Then, what is a noun?

STUDENT 4: Person, place, thing.

By the time the discussion focused on the word *adverbio,* students were able to attend to the teacher's explanation, aided by the process of elimination.

The payoff for making the time and the effort to teach all or most of the time in Spanish is enormous for both the teacher and the students. Teaching in Spanish allows students to experience rapid progress in comprehension and speech production. One first-year Spanish student, for example, was initially very afraid of the speed at which the class was moving. However, she stuck with the immersion course, and her speech began to emerge approximately four weeks into the class. One day she had the following exchange with the instructor:

TEACHER: ¿Cómo estás?

STUDENT: Yo estás mal.

TEACHER: ¿Por qué?

STUDENT: Mi pierna.

TEACHER: ¿Cuál es el problema?

STUDENT: Una chica... wham! (gestures to her leg) mi pierna. Una chica en clase de banda... wham! con la bandera... mi pierna. Yo negro y azul en mi pierna.

(Translation)

TEACHER: How are you?

STUDENT: I are bad.

TEACHER: ¿Why?

STUDENT: My leg.

TEACHER: What's the problem?

STUDENT: A girl . . . wham! (gestures to her leg) my leg. A girl in band class . . . wham! with the flag . . . my leg. I black and blue on my leg.

This beginning language student's ability to sustain a natural, spontaneous conversation despite the lack of specific vocabulary and perfect grammar is typical of beginners who are accustomed to an input-rich environment. She exploited the language she *did* know (body parts, physical states, cognates, etc.) to stay in Spanish rather than switching to English because of the vocabulary she *didn't* know at that time: (*bruise, she hit me with the flagpole; my leg hurts*).

Inevitably, the question of error correction arises—to overtly correct or not to correct? There is no easy answer to this question. In general, our consensus has been to attend to errors in writing in an overt way, but to avoid overt correction of student speech during natural conversational activities. Instead, we include the correct forms in our responses, e.g.,

STUDENT: Yo no comprende la pregunta.

TEACHER: ¿Verdad? Pues, yo sí comprendo la pregunta. Yo la comprendo muy bien. ¡Estudio mi tarea! ¡Ji ji! Pero, no te preocupes. Yo la comprendo y te la explico otra vez. Comprendo tu confusión.

(Translation)

STUDENT: I/you don't understand the question.

TEACHER: ¿Really? Well, I do understand the question. I understand it very well. I study my homework! ¡Ha, ha! But, don't worry. I understand it and I'll explain it to you again. I understand your confusion.

Benchmark Testing

As part of the curriculum redesign at Mundelein, teachers saw assessment as a critical component of the program. We were in agreement that feedback was of little use when it was praise, blame, or vague encouragement *¡Qué bueno! ¡B+! (Great! B+!);¡Estudia más, por favor! (Study more, please!)*. Instead, we recognized that assessment, in order to be worthwhile to our students and to ourselves, had to provide feedback that was highly specific and descriptive of how a student's performance met the department's standards (Wiggins 1997: 24).

As a result of departmental research, discussion, and analysis of student performances captured on video, a working model for benchmark testing of students' oral performance was developed and is now in its third year of use. Beginning with the first-year foreign language program, we test students on their overall communicative competence at the midpoint and at the end of levels one and two. Students are evaluated by teachers from a *different* class; teachers volunteer their prep period over the course of two to three days to do benchmark testing. Testers evaluate students' oral performance on a variety of tasks in three areas: Strategic, Discourse, and Sociolinguistic Competences. Because most first-year students cannot control grammar in their speech during real conversations, they are evaluated on grammatical accuracy only in their writing, not during the benchmark testing.

The evaluator marks the rubric for successful Competences during a five to eight minute visit with each student out of the classroom. In terms of Strategic Competence, the evaluator looks for strategies the student uses during the conversation in order to maintain the flow of communication in Spanish. Linguistic errors do not affect the students' scores unless they interfere with the message. During the midpoint benchmarks, the evaluator begins with a simple warm-up activity/interview to obtain sufficient language to begin to score the student on his/her Discourse Competence. The evaluator weaves a conversation based on topics explored in the chapters up to the date of the test, e.g., *¿Cómo te llamas? ¿Cuál es tu apellido? ¿Cuántos años tienes? ¿Dónde vives? ¿Cómo es tu familia? ¿Qué te gusta hacer los fines de semana? (What's your name? What's your last name? How old are you? Where do you live? What's your family like? What do you like to do on the weekends?)* and so on. Questions are selected at random from a pool of general questions and are used as conversational starters for the purpose of eliciting sufficient language for evaluation purposes.

The evaluator then uses the activity known as *Explain, please* (Lee and VanPatten 1995: 163) to provide feedback on the extent to which students demonstrate their Strategic Competence. The student selects a slip of paper at random from a basket. The slip contains instructions in English such as *Explain a cash register receipt to someone who has never seen one; explain a pointer to someone who has never seen or used one.* Items to explain are chosen specifically to be those vocabulary words that students are not likely to encounter in a first-year class. Why? To provide feedback on how well the student makes the most of the language that s/he does have when faced with a conversation about an unfamiliar topic or which includes unfamiliar vocabulary. We created a pool of some thirty cues for the circumlocution task, with words and phrases such as *wig, hippopotamus, telescope, diving board, graffiti, football helmet,* and the *Oscar,* among others. Evaluators listen, watch carefully, and try to guess the secret cue on the paper the student pulls as s/he tries to explain in Spanish what the cue is. On the rubric, evaluators check the most common strategies students use so that they may see where their strengths are and where they need to develop. Highly competent students are encouraged, if time permits, to pull as many papers as they can explain in order to give the evaluator a larger language sample to assess.

We have revised the end-of-term benchmark test as of this writing. Formerly, students participated in role-play situations. Currently, we are experimenting with a paired activity (similar to the Lee and VanPatten (1995) *Explain please,* activity) in which students give each other instructions for drawing pictures. This *Draw it* task is designed to elicit more evidence of Strategic Competence, given the important role that this aspect of Competence plays in the beginners' overall communicative ability.

Conclusion

Over the past three years, written feedback from our students along with our observations of the obvious rise in Spanish used by students suggest that making Strategic Competence a major goal in our classrooms has had a significant impact on the way we teach, and on the quantity and quality of our students' comprehension and production. In the past, teachers who chose to approximate immersion in the classroom shouldered a major burden for anticipating the comprehension needs of the students. Now, while we continue to stress the importance of immersion, we expect students to share a greater part of the burden for making themselves understood, and for understanding the input coming at them. We provide students with the tools they need by means of linguistic support, comprehensible input in a wide variety of contexts, and summative feedback on tasks that simulate authentic language challenges faced with native speakers. We continually stress that English is not acceptable under most circumstances in the classroom, and we model that behavior. Translation becomes unnecessary and, indeed, counterproductive in that when English is allowed as a viable alternative, students delay their development of Strategic Competence. By teaching to Strategic Compretence, we help students become skilled at defining or describing vocabulary, thereby facilitating thinking in Spanish and facility with the language. Students develop the confidence and language needed to survive in a conversation with native speakers who are not likely to limit conversation topics to those that that have been covered in the student's text.

Recently, we asked a group of third and fourth year students to give us their feedback on the Spanish program at Mundelein High School. We believe their words speak well for the work described in this paper:

> *It amazes me sometimes when one of the teachers talks so fast in Spanish and we understand them [sic]. Especially after taking Spanish for such a short period of time. I got used to hearing Spanish, and now can understand it well. Speaking it is a little more difficult but I am getting better. What I like is how the teachers only speak Spanish. . . the MHS program has taught me that in order to learn something, you must be able to apply it.*

Hear, hear ... (we do!)

References

Krashen, Stephen D., and Terrell, Tracy D. 1983. *The Natural Approach: Language Acquisition in the Classroom.* San Francisco: Alemany Press.

Lee, James F., and VanPatten, Bill. 1995. *Making Communicative Language Teaching Happen.* New York: McGraw-Hill.

Lusser Rico, Gabriele. 1983. *Writing the Natural Way.* Los Angeles: J.P.Tarcher, Inc.

Musumeci, Diane. 1996. "Teacher-Learner Negotiation in Content-Based Instruction: Communication at Cross-Purposes?" *Applied Linguistics* 17, 3 (c).

VanPatten, Bill. 1986. "Second Language Acquisition Research and the Learning/Teaching of Spanish: Some Research Findings and Implications." *Hispania.* 69:1, 202-216.

Wiggins, Grant. 1997. "Practicing What We Preach in Designing Authentic Assessments". *Educational Leadership.* December 1996/January 1997. 18-25.

5
Addressing the Diversity of Learner Abilities Through Strategy Training

Susanne Rott
Purdue University

Margaret Wendling
Clark Middle/High School

Introduction

The current trend to establish learner-centered language programs by making key decisions, namely "*what* will be taught, *how* it will be taught, *when* it will be taught, and *how* it will be assessed" (emphasis added; Nunan 1995: 134) with reference to learners, has been the result of the increasing body of knowledge about learning processes from second language acquisition research and consequently the effort to improve the effectiveness of foreign language classroom instruction. The focus on learners has so far affected areas concerning (a) program goals, (b) classroom practices, and (c) materials used. While on the one hand promoting and providing an atmosphere conducive to language acquisition, on the other hand the learner-centered classroom also creates many difficult challenges which have the potential of discouraging and causing difficulties for the learners. In spite of the need, language instruction has not as of yet been adjusted to include the explicit teaching of strategies to overcome these difficulties.

New program goals of many foreign language (FL) departments are based on learner's development of functional communicative language abilities, i.e., communicative language competence. Savignon (1983) provides a pedagogical approach to communicative competence based on Canale and Swain (1980) which consists of the following components: grammatical competence, which refers to linguistic knowledge including vocabulary, pronunciation, spelling, and sentence structure; sociolinguistic competence, which refers to appropriate usage of language in various contexts to convey specific meaning; discourse competence, which refers to the ability to comprehend and produce one cohesive thought based on a connection of individual sentences; and strategic competence, which refers to the ability to compensate for deficiencies in linguistic knowledge during oral communication. For example, grammatical competence is addressed in the classroom by grammar tasks that focus on the command of syntax and vocabulary; sociolinguistic competence is often enhanced through units which focus on specific cultural issues; discourse competence can be practiced through reading texts as well as open-ended class discussions; and strategic competence is trained by developing students' techniques to continue conversations. Although all four areas are considered necessary for communicative competence, strategic competence has largely been neglected so far.

Pedagogical literature has provided a strong rational for compensatory strategy instruction in conjunction with learning strategy instruction (Oxford 1990 for example). Providing learners with communicative materials and engaging them in nontraditional communicative classroom practices result in the need to equip learners with the tools to use the materials most efficiently. In order to immediately begin the development of the "ability to communicate within restrictions" (Savignon 1983: 43) a coherent and conceptualized approach to strategy instruction is required. This need is not reflected in course goals included on syllabi, nor is it listed in table of contents of textbooks.

In this article we outline the way in which a focus on compensation strategies in the framework of communicative language teaching can accommodate the diversity of learner abilities. To appropriately address classroom tasks, we suggest the concept of compensation strategies be expanded beyond oral communication to all four skill areas, namely reading, writing, listening, and speaking. We then consider the communicative classroom as a setting which creates the need for compensation strategies. Next we present practical classroom application of strategy instruction by looking at learner limitations and possible techniques to overcome them. Finally, we propose the use of strategies when testing.

Expanding the Concept of Compensation Strategies

While the concept of strategic competence initially referred to oral communication strategies and the "imperfect knowledge of rules" (Savignon 1983: 40) only, Oxford and Crookall, for example, have expanded the definition of compensation strategies to "behaviors used to compensate for missing knowledge of *some kind*" (emphasis added; 1989: 404). In their definition the researchers do not restrict the reason for difficulties in communication to linguistic knowledge. They account for research findings, which have elicited a variety of knowledge sources besides linguistic knowledge that can have an impact on the success of communication. Such sources include cultural background, schema, and content knowledge.

Similarly, the communicative aspect of compensation strategies has thus far only been considered for oral communication. Dörnyei (1995), for example, found that compensation strategies for oral communication can be taught and have a significant impact on the quality and quantity of learners' strategy use, and therefore on fluency. His study demonstrated that strategy training regarding circumlocution significantly improved the learners' ability to deal with insufficient vocabulary. Furthermore, a repertoire of fillers, such as "well" and "you know," for different emotions and moods allowed learners to remain in conversations by gaining time.

The development of functional communication ability, however, should refer not only to oral communication but also to written text as well as non-collaborative listening tasks (video and tape recordings) (Oxford, Levine and Crookall 1989). Since the basic premise of communication is an exchange of information, not only speaking, but also reading, writing, and listening, tasks need to be considered communicative due to the fact that a transfer of information occurs. Readers and listeners receive information from written and oral texts, while writers convey information in written form. Communication breakdown can take place if readers and listeners do not comprehend ideas or if writers cannot convey their ideas to their readers. Therefore, compensation strategies are necessary for communication in all four language skills.

Many of the currently used textbooks aim at helping learners to access oral and written texts easier and better by providing preactivities which address learners' linguistic knowledge, extralinguistic knowledge sources (e.g. content and background knowledge), and learners' monitor skills (e.g. skimming and scanning). Yet, these tasks are not labeled as strategies which learners could use independently outside the classroom. Rather, learners perceive pre-activities as "just another" textbook activity and do not recognize their strategic potential; i.e., strategies in the form of preactivities provide only implicit strategy instruction. A strategic approach to language learning and communication aims at actively involving learners in their learning process. Researchers generally agree that the development of strategic language skills requires a conscious and explicit effort on the part of the learner.

Why Teach Compensation Strategies?

In taking a closer look at the communicative teaching/learning environment it becomes clear that learners are placed in a linguistically challenging situation. The need for compensation strategies becomes obvious if instructors make themselves aware of the types of tasks in which they ask the learners to engage. Swaffar, Arens, & Byrnes have described the advances in classroom techniques and materials as the "New Paradigm" (1991:12) of teaching, which in contrast to the "Previous Paradigm" emphasizes the use of authentic texts, integrative use of grammar, independent learning, contextualized language practice, and personalized language use. Under the "New Paradigm" the basic principle of communicative language teaching, namely that learners gain written as well as oral communication skills by engaging in real-life communication, is implemented by encouraging learners to use the target language (TL) to express their ideas and opinions in a variety of situational contexts. Especially at the beginning level where learners' vocabulary and control of structures are limited, these contexts mainly concern issues of daily life about which learners can easily provide information in their native language. The challenge in oral as well as written communication tasks lies in assessing their resources (vocabulary and structures) and consequently managing them most effectively for comprehending as well as communicating ideas in the TL.

Moreover, to maximize (Lee & VanPatten 1995) learners' opportunities for social interaction (Kramsch 1987), most classroom tasks are created to allow for partner and small group work; i.e., all learners are actively involved in completing a task at the same time. Communicative tasks, by nature, require learners throughout the language class to interact with others by comprehending ideas and responding either physically, in written form, or in oral form. Ideally student-student interaction during the task and teacher-student and student-teacher interaction during the follow-up take place in the TL only. Therefore, in order to avoid reverting to their native language, learners need to be aware of techniques and their own resources to solve linguistic impasses and prevent the interruption of information exchange. As a result, learners can assume their "new" role as active "coworkers" (Lee & VanPatten 1995:16) of classroom instruction/learning and take on the responsibility for their learning inside the classroom.

In order to stimulate students' interest and contribute to learners' development of cultural literacy, authentic written and oral texts serve as a basis for tasks in all four language skills. In turn, authentic texts (video and tape recordings) for listening activities are usually faster, contain more unfamiliar vocabulary and structures, are interrupted through false starts, and more likely present more unfamiliar schema to the listener than speech that especially addresses foreign language learners at a particular language learning level. Similarly, authentic written texts (literary and expository) are usually longer and syntactically more complex, and might present content that is more difficult to access and comprehend than graded readers. Although research studies have shown that learners can comprehend information conveyed by an unfamiliar grammatical structure (Lee 1987), successfully infer word meaning during reading (e.g., Bensoussan and Laufer 1984), and experience better text recall facilitated by recognized text schemata (Lee and Riley 1990), learners usually are not aware of their resources and therefore do not take advantage of them.

A number of research studies have explored students' use of language learning strategies (including compensation strategies) as well as their approaches to accomplishing various classroom and other learning tasks. Strategy profiles of successful and less successful learners have suggested that the variety of learners in our classes approach tasks differently with varying degrees of success. In fact, Oxford and Ehrmann have summarized research studies explaining "that there is no single strategy pattern used by effective language learners. [. . . Rather] successful learners use an array of strategies matching those strategies to their own learning style and personality and to the demands of the task (in the context of cultural influences)" (1995:362). The use of strategies has been linked to learner factors such as motivation (Oxford and Nyikos 1989), learning style (Rossi-Le 1989; in Oxford and Ehrmann 1995), gender (e.g. Oxford and Nyikos 1989), and age (Oxford and Ehrmann 1993). Although strategy use appears to be highly individual, researchers have been able to make a distinction between successful and less successful learners agreeing that " [e]ffective language learners know how to use appropriate strategies to reach their learning goals, whereas ineffective learners are less expert in their strategy choice and use" and moreover "use strategies less frequently, [. . .] have a smaller repertoire of strategies, and often do not choose appropriate strategies for the task" (Chamot and Kupper 1989:13).

While a majority of researchers consider the teaching of strategies the logical result of present research findings, others have opposed the idea. Dörnyei, for example, has summarized arguments against the teaching of compensation strategies. Some researchers claim that "strategic competence develops in the speaker's L1 and is freely transferable to target language use" (1995:60). Moreover, they posit that during the course of language study, learners automatically gain sufficient language and flexibility needed to carry out communicative tasks proposing to teach language instead of strategies. However, the question is how long it takes learners to develop the flexibility of strategic language use by themselves and how learners should deal with their limitations until they gain flexibility without losing their motivation to study a foreign language. In addition, as strategy profiles of less successful learners have shown, instructors can not be assured that learners bring effective compensation strategies developed in their first language to the foreign language classroom.

In order to address all learners, successful as well as less successful, provide them with equal learning opportunities, and facilitate them "to make learning easier, faster, more enjoyable, more self-directed, more effective, and more transferable to new situations" (Oxford 1990: 8), compensation strategy training needs to be an integral part of language teaching and learning. Strategy training can motivate learners to accept initial ambiguity, make efficient use of their resources, and consequently handle communicative tasks in all four skill areas with more confidence. Compensation strategy instruction needs to entail the following steps:

1. Students need to be aware that their limitations are common to all language learners. The first step of strategy instruction should be to sensitize learners for the challenges and potential problems they might encounter while accomplishing a specific task. By doing so instructors clarify expectations of task outcome and send the message that learners' problems are taken seriously.

2. Strategy instruction furthermore needs to provide an array of possible strategies (Chamot and Kupper 1989) which learners should practice and evaluate the usefulness for their individual learning styles. In addition, learners need to analyze the effectiveness of strategies they are already using (Chamot and Kupper 1989) and moreover become aware of their linguistic and extralinguistic resources and consequently their strategic abilities.

3. In addition, learners need to perceive strategies as a useful tool to compensate for their language limitations. Since not all strategies work for every language task and all learning styles, learners need to understand that strategy use will not always lead to optimal success but nevertheless should be considered when impasses occur during communication.

4. A strategic approach should be allowed and fostered in oral as well as written exams by awarding points for strategy use.

Integrating Strategy Instruction in Daily Lesson Plans

In the following pages we have outlined some possible step-by-step applications of strategy training that can easily be integrated in daily lesson plans. Each strategy training description points out the learner limitations which can be compensated for by the strategy. During the last step of strategy training students ask themselves whether the strategy helped them to accomplish the task and overcome their limitation and whether they would consider using the strategy again. If not, the students are encouraged to assess whether the lack of success was due to the nature of the task or to their own learning preferences. It is then suggested to learners to try another strategy which might work better for them. Some of the strategies presented below are used in classrooms as games or textbook activities but are not explicitly introduced as potential strategies that can be transferred to other tasks. Such a conceptualized introduction is required.

Reading Tasks

Possible Learner Limitations

When learners are confronted with an authentic reading text they often feel overwhelmed and defeated before even attempting the task. These feelings are due to the length and unrecognizable vocabulary of the text. Students neglect to apply their own knowledge, which could help them to comprehend the text more easily, do not make use of the context they do recognize in order to infer word meaning, or do not approach the text for its global meaning. This initial fear and limited perspective can be overcome if the learners get accustomed to applying the following strategies:

(a) Word Inferencing. When presented with an authentic text, learners encounter unfamiliar vocabulary which is perceived as essential for text comprehension. Looking up each unfamiliar word in the dictionary slows down the reading process and results in the comprehension of individual words but not in comprehension of the larger concept or ideas of the text. Rather, learners should become accustomed to inferring the meaning of words from context. This can be demonstrated to the learners through the following game in the TL:

1. Each pair of students receives five short reading passages each containing one nonsense word.
2. Students try to infer the meaning from its context as quickly as possible. The first group to get all five nonsense words correct wins.
3. After the game learners should share which textual clues helped them to make meaning of the unfamiliar words. In addition, learners identity where context did not provide sufficient hints to make an inference. That way, learners realize that the strategy can but does not always lead to success.

Another way to approach the training of word inferencing:

1. Learners individually skim the text to be read and underline all unfamiliar words.
2. With a partner they try to infer meaning using contextual clues.
3. Learners report about their success and failure to infer meaning. At this point learners will realize that this strategy works in some contexts but not in others.
4. After reading the text for meaning and identifying the main ideas, the class should also discuss whether all the words they underlined as unfamiliar were essential to comprehend the main ideas. The goal is that learners realize that explicit word knowledge of all of the words they

identified as unfamiliar for comprehension was not essential for global text comprehension. That way learners might feel less overwhelmed by unfamiliar words during future reading activities.

(b) Scanning. Learners often feel inhibited by the abundance of information they receive when reading authentic texts. Instead of reading for the general gist, learners can identify in advance the specific information they expect to gain from the text and focus their attention during reading. This strategy is best used for texts from which specific information needs to be elicited, such as apartment ads. Moreover, the strategy can also help to compensate for time constraints.

1. Before reading the text, learners first read the questions and note key words in order to anticipate ideas they will find in the text.
2. Learners scan the text to locate ideas and key words derived from the questions. It is important that learners make sure that what they anticipated is in fact in the text! In order to evaluate the effectiveness of this strategy and point out that the strategy does not work for every text, learners should determine whether or not they were able to anticipate correctly.
3. Learners read the text and answer the questions.

(c) Management. This strategy helps learners to overcome attention span limitations and cope with the abundance of information presented in longer texts. By summarizing main ideas while reading multi-paragraph texts, learners are actively involved in text comprehension, get a better picture of the text as a whole, and consequently feel more comfortable and in control of the text.

1. The learners are presented with a text for which they write key words, phrases, or short summaries next to each paragraph. This can be done in the TL or in learners' native language.
2. Learners read the questions to the text and identify in which paragraph (already numbered by the instructor) they expect to find the answers according to the key words, phrases, and summaries they have written.
3. To answer the questions to the text learners read individual paragraphs for details.
4. After reading the text again and answering the questions, learners check to see if the answers were found in the paragraphs they predicted. As a final step, learners establish whether or not this strategy facilitated coping with a multi-paragraph text and whether they will use this strategy again.

(d) Awareness. The following strategy also helps learners to cope with longer texts and compensates for attention span limitations. Beginning learners especially are often overwhelmed with the many tasks that are involved in a reading activity (e.g., identify characters and words, string them together, assign and interpret meaning). In a case in which learners are asked to read longer texts, they often have difficulty following the "story." In fact, many learners claim to have "read" a text although they are unable to recall the main ideas, discuss the text, or express their opinions about it. Active text comprehension at all times can help in keeping the reader on track and conscious of the "story." This active comprehension consists of the reader keeping in mind questions such as, What does this text mean to me? What is new for me? What did I learn about the target culture? while reading the passage. After reading a text, learners should always think about and answer these questions for themselves (in the TL or in their native language). Connecting text information to their own knowledge and experiences makes the text more meaningful and memorable for the learners.

(e) Schema and Background Knowledge Activation. Learners bring their own knowledge to the text, which can be helpful for text comprehension and to compensate for unfamiliar vocabulary. This knowledge can be activated and made available by associating background knowledge with a picture or a title and subtitles which accompany the text. The learners' schema about a topic is not always exactly the same to that which is presented in the text. This can mislead the learners' comprehension if they do not actively check whether the information they expect can really be found in the text! After all, a target language text should always present some new information to the learners.

1. In pairs, learners look at a picture or title for which they write down words or phrases they associate with the picture or title.
2. The instructor collects the ideas on the overhead in the form of a list.
3. Learners read the text.
4. As a class, learners check whether the anticipated ideas were really in the text. Ideas that are in the text are checked off, ideas that are not in the text are crossed out. The instructor points out that students should apply their own knowledge to the text but that it is not always appropriate. Therefore, they always need to check and confirm their hypotheses during reading.

Writing Tasks

Possible Learner Limitations

When writing in a foreign language, learners are often frustrated because they cannot express themselves as accurately and easily as they can in their native language. Learners often think in their native language and tend to translate word for word into the foreign language. Since they often lack vocabulary or have difficulty retrieving the vocabulary needed to express their ideas, they try to compensate with vocabulary from their native language or produce incoherent sentences. In order to overcome these hindrances and function most effectively in the foreign language during writing, learners can use the following strategies:

(a) Circumlocution. Learners try to describe (define, explain) the unknown word with the vocabulary they know in order to convey their message. The strategy can be introduced and trained in the following manner:

1. The instructor displays a set of pictures on the overhead for which the vocabulary is known and gathers all the vocabulary items the students associate with the pictures.
2. The instructor models this strategy by writing a description of one of the vocabulary items on the overhead, e.g., the instructor chooses *Urlaub* (vacation) and describes it as *keine Arbeit* (not going to work), *wegfahren* (leave town).
3. The learners write their own circumlocutions of other vocabulary items with partners in much the same way.
4. Some learners present their circumlocutions to the class. The other learners guess which word is being described. At this point the learners can monitor the comprehensibility of their circumlocution depending on whether or not they are understood by classmates.
5. The learners use their circumlocutions in order to write a short story with their partners. The instructor models the first sentence again, e.g., *Nächste Woche arbeite ich nicht, ich fahre weg* (Next week I will not work, I will go out of town).
6. A few of the final products are presented to the classmates.

(b) Changing and Revising an Idea. Prior to actually beginning to write a text or an essay, learners need to check and see whether they know the vocabulary necessary to express themselves. They can do this by brainstorming their ideas and the necessary vocabulary in the TL. This strategy can improve the flow of the writing process because learners do not have to switch back and forth between languages. Furthermore, it prevents learners from starting to write ideas they are unable to complete due to lack of vocabulary. The strategy can be demonstrated and practiced in class by brainstorming with the learners as in the following activity:

1. The instructor presents a topic to the learners.
2. The learners brainstorm in small groups and write down related words and phrases in the TL. By getting into the TL mode, word-for-word translation can also be avoided during the writing process.

3. The instructor collects the ideas on the overhead. This way learners also realize the abundance of ideas they can express in the TL without reverting to English.

4. The whole class writes a story together using selected ideas from the brainstorming activity which the instructor writes on the overhead.

5. The learners carry out this process over a 1–2 week period, gradually working more and more independently. That is, the next time the learners write in pairs and then at home on their own. Finally, the whole process should be done independently.

Oral Tasks

Possible Learner Limitations

Speaking in a foreign language causes many problems and fears for some learners as they must understand (recognize, interpret, and make sense of sounds) and formulate ideas and retrieve vocabulary and structures on the spot. By learning and using tools which allow them to be more flexible in conversation, the learners can compensate for their deficiencies. The learners can do so by using the following strategies:

(a) Circumlocution. This strategy was already explained for the skill of writing.

(b) Request Assistance. In a situation where the learner has difficulty continuing the conversation, certain learned phrases can prove to be helpful. Introducing these phrases through visual aids such as a video can prove to be entertaining, interesting, and have a lasting effect on the learners. Following the steps below is one way of introducing this strategy to the learners:

1. Learners receive a worksheet with helpful phrases, such as *Können Sie bitte lauter sprechen? Wiederholen Sie das, bitte.* (Could you please speak a little louder? Could you please repeat that?), which the instructor explains.

2. Learners watch a video and identify how these phrases are responded to and what purpose they serve. The video can be a sampling of short scenes from authentic TV series.

3. The responses, purpose, and effectiveness are discussed with the instructor. The instructor points out that using these phrases is not negative nor is it merely demonstrating an inability to understand something. Rather, it is positive, demonstrates flexibility, and often results in a better understanding of the subject at hand.

4. The next day the instructor begins speaking very rapidly in the TL expecting the learners to respond with the introduced phrases. If the teacher responds by speaking more slowly, students realize that the strategy indeed works.

5. The use of this strategy is encouraged in learner-instructor and learner-learner conversations during class and when taking oral exams.

(c) Pool Ideas. In a role-play situation with a limited amount of time to prepare a dialogue with a partner, brainstorming can aid in sharing and pooling ideas assuring that each learner is familiar with possible topics and can anticipate the direction the conversation is headed. In addition, learners prepare basic questions that can lead the conversation into the next topic. The learners can use any of the pooled ideas in the conversation. Such an activity often results in a continuing conversation, as it is more free and flexible. During the role play the learners can focus on conversing and not on coming up with ideas or searching for vocabulary. This strategy can be practiced in class in the following way:

1. Learners are presented with a topic: *Stellen Sie sich vor: Heute ist der erste Unitag nach den Semesterferien. Sie treffen Freunde in der Mensa. Unterhalten Sie sich.* (Imagine today is your first day at the university. You meet friends in the cafeteria. Make a dialogue.)

2. The learners come up with possible ideas, questions, and topics which are collected on the overhead. For example: *Wie geht's? Urlaub, Strand, Berge.* (How are you? vacation, beach, mountains). Learners should only write their ideas and not an outline of a dialogue which they try to memorize.

3. At this point, it is important for the instructor to point out the fact that the learners can use ideas from other members of their group and not only the ideas they came up with. It is also good to emphasize the fact that cooperation with group members leads to a multitude of ideas and options which they would not have had if they had worked on their own.

4. Learners split into groups and create dialogues using the pooled ideas. The dialogues are then presented to the class. Learners are made aware of the flexibility gained through the use of this strategy through class discussion of ideas included in the dialogues.

Listening Tasks

Possible Learner Limitations

In listening comprehension activities which expose the students to authentic language, learners often get distracted or frustrated by unknown or unrecognized vocabulary, fragmented sentences, and fast-paced speech. Such problems can be reduced by a variety of strategic behaviors.

(a) Focused Listening. In order to familiarize themselves with the content of the dialogue and focus on the specific details or aspects needed from the dialogue, learners are better prepared if they read the questions before listening to an authentic text. This is important because listening to the dialogue and reading the questions at the same time is extremely demanding on the learners. The key words of these questions should be kept in mind throughout the listening activity. The following activity is a way to practice this:

1. In order to demonstrate the validity of this strategy, the learners listen to the dialogue and try to answer the questions without having read the questions beforehand. Most learners will not be able to simultaneously listen, read, and focus on the important aspects of the dialogue.

2. The instructor gives the learners the opportunity to familiarize themselves with the content of the questions that accompany a listening activity.

3. The instructor points out that the learners should underline what they consider to be key words of the questions. By doing this, each learner is actively and consciously involved with the task.

4. Keeping the key words in mind, the learners listen to the text and answer the questions individually.

5. The instructor goes over the questions and answers with the learners.

(b) Activation of Vocabulary Knowledge. Another way of preparing for listening comprehension tasks is to specifically retrieve the vocabulary that is anticipated in a certain situation. For example: *Wegbeschreibung* (giving/receivingdirections)

1. In order to show the usefulness of this strategy, the instructor first reads a set of directions without having activated the necessary vocabulary. (Chances are, learners will be baffled.)

2. The instructor presents the learners with a set of pictures which corresponds to the topic.

3. As a class, learners identify the vocabulary items in the pictures. (This can also be done by asking the learners to identify the vocabulary they associate with giving directions.)

4. The directions are read. Learners follow the path on the map.

5. The instructor draws the students' attention to the increase in comprehension of the instructions when the vocabulary is first activated.

(c) Activation of Discourse Structure. Dialogues in routine situations often follow discourse patterns that can easily be anticipated. Anticipating the flow of such a dialogue can simplify the learners' approach to the task. This can be done by determining appropriate questions which usually arise given a particular situation. This strategy can be introduced in the following manner:

1. The instructor writes the title/place in which the dialogue occurs on the overhead. For example: Am *Fahrkartenschalter* (buying a train ticket).

2. In pairs, learners create questions which they anticipate might be asked by the sales agent.

3. The instructor collects the suggested questions on the overhead.

4. The dialogue is played.

5. The learners answer the questions they posed according to the information in the dialogue.

6. The instructor points out the fact that given only minimal information, the learners were able to anticipate the direction and content of the dialogue. This makes the task easier as the learners have already activated their knowledge of the content and the vocabulary of the dialogue before actually listening to it. Of course this activity could also prove that learners were not able to activate the appropriate discourse structure because of a culture-specific discourse structure. Again, the instructor needs to point out that learners need to confirm or discard their hypothesis when listening to the tape.

Integrating Strategies in Tests

Compensation strategies can and need to be integrated in testing. Exams in a coherent and well conceptualized language program test what has been taught in class. Logically, exam tasks confront learners with similarly challenging materials which require compensation for linguistic and processing limitations. Allowing and facilitating learners to compensate for their limitations seems only appropriate for learner-centered testing, and, in addition, gives learners an incentive to practice and evaluate strategies on their own.

Testing Vocabulary. While we know that not all learners have an active command of the vocabulary presented during a certain chapter, we should allow learners to compensate for limited word knowledge. This can be done, e.g., by presenting them with a picture containing fifteen lexical items pertaining to a topic or semantic field and asking them to identify only ten.

Testing Listening Comprehension. As already pointed out, learners benefit if they can focus their attention on specific information while listening to a text. Learners, therefore, should read the questions or statements to a listening task before actually hearing the text. That way, they do not have to read and listen at the same time, can familiarize themselves with the vocabulary, and can anticipate what they might hear in the text.

Testing Reading Comprehension. The management strategy which helps learners to compensate for attention span limitations can easily be used for testing. Learners can be asked to supply a summary sentence to every paragraph read. This should be done in the students' native language so that their limited TL writing skills do not interfere. Another possibility is to provide learners with a list of summary sentences in scrambled order which learners have to match with the appropriate paragraphs.

Testing Writing. Brainstorming of ideas in the TL to check whether learners know the appropriate words to express their thoughts can easily be added as the pre-activity to a writing task.

Testing Oral Communication. During oral exams learners should be encouraged and receive extra credit if they indicate that they have not understood their interlocutor and request clarification (instead of simply switching to their native language or not responding to their interlocutor's message).

Conclusion

In this essay, we demonstrated that the effectiveness of learner-centered communicative classroom language learning depends largely on learners' ability to cope with comprehension and production limitations, i.e., learners need compensation strategies to minimize linguistic impasses and prevent communication breakdown. We extended the conceptualization of compensation strategies to reading, writing, and listening to account for communication problems in all four skill areas.

Providing learners with an array of tools and techniques for compensation is particularly important because communicative language teaching stresses learners' active involvement in their language learning process and the development of communication skills they can use independently of teacher and textbook. Moreover, compensation strategies can contribute indirectly to learners' language development in that they prevent communication breakdown and at the same time increase the quantity of students' interaction with other speakers and materials.

Compensation strategy training allows instructors to address the diverse learning abilities of students in their classes. Pointing out the variety of problems learners might encounter when engaging in oral and written TL tasks and explaining effective and less effective approaches to solving linguistic impasses helps learners establish realistic expectations of task outcomes. Furthermore, compensation strategy training motivates learners to build on and make use of their linguistic (e.g., circumlocution and brainstorming) and extra-linguistic resources (e.g., schema knowledge and management strategy) as well as their monitor skills (e.g., management and changing and revising an idea). That way, learners' individual abilities become an important part of their language learning experience.

The key to the successful integration of compensation strategies is awareness. Learners as well as instructors need to be aware for the challenge each language task posits. In addition, learners need to understand the usefulness of compensation strategies by practicing individual strategies and gaining experience in evaluating the strategy's effectiveness. Instructors, on the other hand, need to be aware of the long-term developmental process that learners go through while identifying the appropriate strategies that fit their learning style.

Through the examples we hoped to show that the introduction of compensation strategies to learners can easily be integrated in daily lesson plans as well as in testing. The list of strategies presented above is not exhaustive, but it does provide novice teachers with a solid repertoire to which they can refer.

References

Bensoussan, M., and Laufer, B. 1994. "Lexical Guessing in Context in EFL Reading Comprehension." *Journal of Research in Reading* 7: 15-32.

Canale, M., and Swain, M. 1980. "Theoretical Basis of Communicative Approaches to Teaching and Testing." *Applied Linguistics* 1: 1-47.

Chamot, A. U., and Kupper, L. 1989. "Learning Strategies in Foreign Language Instruction." *Foreign Language Annals* 22: 13-24.

Dörnyei, Z. 1995. "On the Teachability of Communication Strategies." *TESOL Quarterly* 29: 55-85.

Kramsch, C. J. 1987. "Interactive Discourse in Small and Large Groups." In W. M. Rivers (Ed.), *Interactive Language Teaching,* 17-32. Cambridge: Cambridge University Press.

Lee, J. 1987. "Comprehending the Spanish Subjunctive: An Information Processing Perspective". *Modern Language Journal* 71: 50-57.

Lee, J., and Riley, G.L. 1990. "The Effect of Prereading, Rhetorically-Oriented Frameworks on the Recall of Two Structurally Different Expository Texts." *Studies in Second Language Acquisition* 12: 25-41.

Lee, J., and VanPatten, B. 1995. *Making Communicative Language Teaching Happen*. New York: McGraw Hill.

Nunan, D. 1995. "Closing the Gap Between Learning and Instruction." *TESOL Quarterly* 29:133-158.

Oxford, R. 1990. *Language Learning Strategies: What Every Teacher Should Know*. New York: Newbury House.

Oxford, R. and Crookall, D. 1989. "Research on Language Learning Strategies: Methods, Findings, and Instructional Issues." *Modern Language Journal* 73: 404-419.

Oxford, R., and Ehrmann, M. 1993. "Second Language Research on Individual Differences" *Annual Review of Applied Linguistics* 23: 188-205.

Oxford, R., and Ehrmann, M. 1995. "Adults' Language Learning Strategies in an Intensive Foreign Language Program in the United States." *System* 23: 359-386.

Oxford, R., Lavine, R. Z., and Crookall, D. 1989. "Language Learning Strategies, the Communicative Approach, and their Classroom Implications." *Foreign Language Annals* 22: 29-39.

Oxford, R., and Nyikos, M. 1989. "Variables Affecting Choice of Language Learning Strategies by University Students." *Modern Language Journal* 73: 291-300.

Savignon, S. J. 1983. *Communicative Competence: Theory and Classroom Practice. Texts and Contexts in Second Language Learning*. Reading, MA: Addison Wesley.

Swaffar, J., Arens, K., and Byrnes, H. 1991. *Reading for Meaning: An Integrated Approach to Language Learning*. Englewood Cliffs, NJ: Prentice Hall.

6
Teaching Language and Culture Beyond the Classroom Walls

Scott Barkhurst
Bucyrus High School

Judith W. Failoni
Fontbonne College

The goals of the ACTFL Standards for Foreign Language Learning involve language and culture in a broad sense, with a connection to other disciplines and participation in the community. Unfortunately, the focus of foreign language learning has often centered on students' activities in the classroom with little opportunity to include the wider school and civic community. To meet the Standards, instruction should extend beyond the classroom setting with activities designed to reach a larger audience, yet reinforce what is happening in the foreign language classroom.

The performing arts project briefly described in this article will demonstrate the concept of meaningful extracurricular undertakings and how cultural literacy and language learning can be evaluated in a nontraditional setting. Although goal-oriented extracurricular projects like this have been undertaken successfully for many years at the author's high school, one specific interdisciplinary French project will be used as a model with suggestions for general application to any language and any level. This project provided an approach to the teaching of the language and culture through the presentation of a theatrical performance, complete with an authentic meal, music, and dance, using the performing arts as a learning tool. As Morain (1983) suggested, the best way to teach culture is through cognitive and affective aspects involving students in audio, visual, verbal, and behavioral experiences.

The psychological basis for the multisensory approach is the theory of multiple intelligences codified by Howard Gardner (1983, 1993). This theory states that all humans have varying degrees of at least seven intelligences: linguistic, logical-mathematical, spatial, musical, bodily-kinesthetic, interpersonal, and intrapersonal. The extracurricular performance project described here is a blend of all of these intelligences. Obviously the musical, linguistic, and bodily-kinesthetic intelligences were utilized in the actual performance. Logical-mathematical intelligence was used in the research and plan for the show. The spatial intelligence was used in set design. Interpersonal and linguistic intelligences were merged with the roles of waiters, narrators, hosts, and ushers. The intrapersonal intelligence was cultivated in two ways: (1) through a self-reflection in which the student examined his/her own feelings about the target culture, and (2) through a realization of another culture when enacting the songs and dramatic situations. Students had options regarding levels and types of participation, and as Theisen states, "… the learner's preferred intelligences will emerge in student-initiated activities where there is a choice in creating a product or solving a problem" (1977: 5).

Activities that are multisensory satisfy the Standards for Foreign Language Learning in unique ways, accommodating diverse learning styles and special needs (Theisen, 1997). Although methodology literature in the past has focused on songs to aid in linguistic endeavors or as cultural activities (Abrate 1988, 1992; Failoni 1993; Hamblin 1987), it is the active, hands-on experiences that foster retention of concepts. The few articles encouraging the incorporation of drama in the foreign language classroom, often opera or videos, usually assume that the student is a responder to the musical or dramatic stimulus, requiring more of a passive role as listener (Vialet 1992). Instead, the project described in the following pages allowed students the opportunity to actually perform the material, creating an atmosphere in which the students were actively involved in the learning process. Students participated by doing, not only by reading, listening, speaking and writing. Through this multisensory extracurricular experience, students used their intelligences for problem solving and creative thinking, exploring language and culture outside the normal confines of books and the formal classroom.

Objectives of the Activity

The major goal that drives the extracurricular program should be linguistic gain and cultural literacy in an interrelated activity involving the community. Classroom reading, writing, listening, and speaking are not enough to give the students an adequate understanding of the language and culture, because a language is more than just a spoken word. It conveys the way of life for the people who live that particular language. Language and culture taught simultaneously allow the basic sociological ideas of people's lifestyles, attitudes, aspirations, history, and tribulations to help provide cultural literacy.

Students must be able to experience firsthand how different people live, because simply reading about it or listening to music is not as powerful. Although trips or exchanges may be the ultimate cultural experience, trips are costly. Therefore, this performance project is especially important in creating experiences of a different culture when the student lives and goes to school in a community that lacks diversity and funds to travel. The project described below closes the gap between the book and the living culture in a different way. The performance takes place out of the normal classroom situation and can simulate authentic situations, not just role play as is likely in the classroom.

Often, attempts at performance productions outside the classroom result in entertainment with little teaching value and without a plan to evaluate the success of cultural and linguistic goals. By carefully designing behavioral objectives and evaluation processes, the project will have meaningful value. Three objectives of the project described here incorporated the following outcomes: (1) the students would achieve linguistic skills within the cultural context associated with the language, (2) the students would use the performing arts as a means to learn the language and the culture, (3) the students would use culture and the performing arts to involve other students and the community. By constructing evaluation guidelines, teachers would be able to assess the learning outcomes and be assured that the extracurricular activity has academic as well as affective merit.

Sample Project

The following brief overview of one performing arts project will present an idea of the type of material used and an evaluation process with suggestions for further development. This extracurricular project was created in a public high school in a midwestern, industry-based town of about 14,000 people. About 650 students attend the high school, but only about 15% of the graduates continue to a four-year college. A large number of students qualify for the reduced or free lunch program. Two languages are offered, with four levels each, and one teacher for each language. About half of the student body take a foreign language in any given year.

French students are encouraged to participate in the extracurricular project every year, but it is not a requirement. Most French students participate, as well as many students who are not taking French. In the particular project discussed here, 127 students were involved in some facet; 108 of them were French students. The performing arts project takes place for three evenings in the high school cafeteria with tables and chairs arranged in a dinner theater format. About 600 to 650 people attend, with tickets sold to cover the cost of the food and other aspects of the production. The program is advertised in school and by the local media.

Throughout all the planning, the task of the teacher lies in taking performance material and turning it into a learning situation and interesting theater. The teacher for this model project chose selections and the students researched the songs, cultural points, and historical figures. One danger with such a large project is underestimating the cooperation and time needed for planning and rehearsing. Class time was not used for rehearsing, so careful scheduling of space and time was crucial.

Major problems with performance shows of this type included finding suitable music with available sheet music or instrumental tape. Inquiries must be made to publishers regarding copyright policies. The performance ability of students is also a determining factor of the program, as students wanted to feel good about the final product and promote a positive image. This interdisciplinary performance involved many departments and other faculty, as accompanists, vocal and dance coaches, set builders, managers, and cooks. Students helped with sets, costumes, props, the dinner, publicity, ticket sales, and worked behind the scenes before and during the show.

In order to create a milieu for authentic experiences, the project should not be just a collection of songs, but rather it should be coordinated around a theme like history, geography, artist, or style. An important factor to consider is who the audience will be. French teachers, for example, will need to decide whether an all French program is suitable or whether a combination of French language performances and English language materials would be better. Due to the audience of various ages consisting of students, parents, and other community members, this project described here successfully included French folk songs, familiar French folk songs sung in English, popular French songs, and selections from French and English musicals and operas.

For this high school project, the theme for selecting the performance pieces was to show certain historical events in chronological order (see Appendix A for a complete program). Beginning in the Middle Ages, the show opened with a number from the American musical *Pippin,* about the son of Charlemagne. The time period then jumped to the French Revolution. One of the cultural aspects here was to show the social strata of French society during this period. The French rock opera, *La Révolution française,* written for the bicentennial of the revolution, tells the story through various musical styles and characters. Two songs were used, one about les Etats généraux that showed the different classes and their views on contemporary French life. This piece includes Louis XVI, nobles, clergy, and le tiers etat, each group with its own distinctive and descriptive music. The second was "La Déclaration des droits de l'homme et du citoyen," equivalent to the American Declaration of Independence. These songs were performed in French and their dramatic impact was to be in the manner in which they were portrayed by the students. The show remained in the eighteenth century with *Candide,* Voltaire's work in musical form by Leonard Bernstein. Two numbers in English gave the students a chance to experience Voltaire's satire of the French society at this time.

Selections from *Les Misérables,* based on Victor Hugo's novel, but sung in English, conveyed the sense of hopelessness and poverty during the early nineteenth century in France. This song gave students the opportunity to become the workers of this era and portray the mood of the text and to match the pounding rhythm and frantic pace of the music. They were therefore not just singing the songs of the period, but reliving them.

> "At the End of the Day"
>
> At the end of the day you're another day older.
>
> And that's all you can say for the life of the poor.
>
> It's a struggle, it's a war.
>
> And there's nothing that anyone's giving.
>
> One more day standing about, what is it for?
>
> One less day to be living.
>
> At the end of the day you're another day colder.
>
> And the shirt on your back doesn't keep out the chill.
>
> And the righteous hurry past,
>
> They don't hear the little ones crying.
>
> And the winter is coming on fast, ready to kill.
>
> One day nearer to dying. (etc.)

Contrasting with the revolution era was the fantasy and drama portrayed in *Phantom of the Opera,* an English opera with a Parisian theme. The French dance, can-can, was performed as authentically and aesthetically as possible, portraying a lighter side of life.

The show moved into the twentieth century with medleys of songs from various eras. Artists such as Maurice Chevalier and Edith Piaf were recognizable through signature songs and reflected an image of France so important in understanding the twentieth century. Included in the pop music scene were two songs by Jacques Brel sung in English. The show concluded with a rousing rendition of the French National Anthem, "La Marseillaise," performed by students with an unfurling of the French tricolor, followed by the universal appeal of Brel's "If We Only Have Love."

A student folk song group appeared throughout the program. Through the group's acting, the audience was able to understand the main idea and cultural importance of various songs. Those songs included the medieval French drinking song, "Chevalier de la Table Ronde," sung in French. With "Frère Jacques," students encouraged the audience to join in, and it gave the students an opportunity to teach what they had learned. "Alouette" was another acted-out folk song (Canadian) that allowed the audience to participate.

Evaluation

Evaluation of the project described above was multifaceted to cover the linguistic, cultural, and community goals. Because the participation for French students was optional, there was no impact on a student's grade in French. However, the teacher did make connections in class with each level of language study and the extracurricular project taking place. Discussions in class and linguistic activities often centered around topics from the program. For example, in the third-year class, the students were studying the conditional tense at the time of the program and performed oral and written activities with questions such as, "Si vous pouviez choisir une de ces chansons de chanter, quelle chanson chanteriez-vous?"

The evaluation of the linguistic gain from the project consisted of students taping themselves reading and speaking at the beginning of the project, and then being taped by the teacher at the end. Although a specific guide was not developed, the teacher believed that greater fluency was achieved as well as confidence. Additionally, the students were taught to sing with correct pronunciation and understanding of the text and practiced correctly their roles as waiter, host, and greeter. During the performances, the teacher observed that students sang correctly, and used appropriate phrases with correct pronunciation in greeting the guests and in serving them.

The teacher also observed that the students tended to be more excited when learning French phrases and vocabulary that had some point to them. As Omaggio (1986) hypothesized, true proficiency-oriented activities provide opportunities to learn language in context and let students apply their knowledge with authentic language-use situations. As an example, the vocabulary and comprehension of "La Marseillaise" came much easier and was much less tedious than if it had been done in the classroom. One year later, the teacher also observed that students were able to recite sections of "La Déclaration des droits de l'homme et du citoyen" from *La Révolution française,* a vivid example of the musical and bodily-kinesthetic intelligences at work.

A second form of evaluation included the pretest/posttest taken by the students involved in the production (see Appendix B for a sample test). The test covered basic facts about France, its culture, and some of the items that they would become familiar with during the course of this particular show. Though brief, it gave an idea about how much students knew about some aspects of French culture before the show and if they retained information afterwards. All students took both tests, even if they were not French students. In the above project, the posttest results showed significant cultural knowledge gain in that students could more accurately answer the questions and could elaborate on certain cultural topics.

Interestingly, the teacher noted that the carryover from the show to the classroom was most enthusiastic. The students realized to a better extent that the French language was not just a grammatical exercise, but was the basic mode of communication of a totally different lifestyle other than their own. Unfortunately, aesthetic response is hard to measure, and the pretest and posttest only assessed facts and knowledge, not deeper emotions or subtle cultural differences. But some of the overall effects could be seen by the teacher as he watched students enact songs, not only producing correct French pronunciation, but also portraying characters and situations from history, appearing to have a greater empathy for what the French have experienced in various time periods. The learning experience was for students to delve into the language and feel through song and theatricalism how the French people might have felt during various periods of history.

The third evaluation of this project assessed the involvement of the community, since the outside world is given the opportunity to see what students have accomplished. From the number of tickets sold and donations from the community, it could be judged that the community valued this type of student presentation. The project displayed the value of successful language learning and helped promote cultural understanding throughout the community, and along with that, the activity promoted the foreign language program in a positive way. All of this benefits the foreign language program, especially in areas without cultural diversity and funds for travel.

Suggestions for Future Activities

Since each performing arts extracurricular project would be a unique experience, teachers need to investigate the school and community resources for other funding sources, such as selling advertisements for the program booklet to help defray costs. A survey of patrons in attendance could help provide a more concrete evaluation of community response. A more exact rubric for linguistic assessment could be devised based on each school's instructional goals. Advanced students could develop intrapersonal intelligence with journal reflections on program topics, exploring their attitudes about cultural or historical situations.

The thematic possibilities for organizing an extracurricular project are endless. Successful theatrical projects have centered around Mardi Gras or other holidays. Geographical regions of France have been another theme, with the inclusion of "Songs from the Auvergne," sung in English or French, and other folk songs reflecting different areas. Historical situations can be brought to life by the performance project. As demonstrated in the project above, figures from the Middle Ages and the revolution years are portrayed in many accessible music or drama forms. In addition, characters such as Joan of Arc or Napoleon have been portrayed in material ready to be incorporated into a show.

La Révolution française could be expanded into a whole show built around this rock opera about the revolution. This opera contains many characters each portrayed in different music styles, which would help the students and audience keep track of what is happening during the performance. This opera includes the children of Louis XVI and Marie Antoinette, portrayed here as a mother rather than the negative image one usually associates with her. Part of the importance of this opera is that it shows the human perspective of the revolution, not just a historical one.

A poem like "Cé" (written by Aragon and set to music by Poulenc in the twentieth century) is a powerful expression of war, with the geographical reference to the bridge at Ce, and historical in the connection of these bridges to the Gaul's defeat by Rome in 51 B.C. and the French defeat in 1940 by Germany. Linguistically, the poem is a good example of the "é" sound and it rhymes throughout. Other language activities could be built around the variety of spellings for the "é" sound, agreement of adjectives and nouns, and use of the past participle.

Cé

J'ai traverse les ponts de Cé
C'est la que tout a commencé
Une chanson des temps passés
Parlé d'un chevalier blessé
D'une rose sur la chaussée
Et d'un corsage délacé
Du château d'un duc insensé
Et des cygnes dans les fossés
De la prairie ou vient danser
Une éternelle fiancée
Et j'ai bu comme un lait glacé
Le long lai des gloires faussées
Le Loire emporté mes pensées
Avec les voitures versées
Et les armes desamorcées
Et les larmes mal effacées
Ô ma France, ô ma délaissée
J'ai traversé les ponts de Cé.

Another thematic idea would be promoting the entire francophone world with representative material from various countries and including music styles different from Western Europe and North America. The display and use of instruments from francophone countries would add authenticity and further educate the larger community. Simple instruments from many parts of the world can be obtained and used as percussion accompanying the music. Songs like "Mon Ile" about la Réunion off the coast of Africa is descriptive and would be easy to coordinate with visuals. This rarely visited part of the francophone world would stimulate many learning activities. In addition, a program focusing on the francophone world could include the Cajun music of Louisiana (readily available in music stores), New England French roots as depicted by singer Josée Vachon, the Caribbean rhythms found in the songs of La Compagnie Créole, and music by francophone groups from North Africa. Dance could be a major component.

An entire performance project could center around Quebec. Besides the wealth of popular music in the last decade and the current popularity of singers like Céline Dion, the songs of the French Voyageurs, travelers on the Canadian river system, provide history and humor about the region. Their songs are very rhythmic and lend themselves to a lot of movement. The fast-paced folk song "Mon Merle" provides a welcome relief to the often over-done "Alouette" and has many linguistic and vocabulary possibilities.

Mon Merle (My Blackbird)

1. Mon merle a perdu son bec, mon merle a perdu son bec.

   Un bec, deux becs, trois becs, marlo.

2. Mon merle a perdu son oeil, mon merle a perdu son oeil.

   Un oeil, deux yeux, trois yeux,

   Un bec, deux becs, trois becs, marlo.

3. Mon merle a perdu sa tête, mon merle a perdu sa tête.

   Une tête, deux têtes, trois têtes,

   Un oeil, deux yeux, trois yeux,

   Un bec, deux becs, trois becs, marlo. (etc.)

Another approach to a performance project would be to focus on the literary arts. Depending on the sophistication and maturity level of the students and audience, favorite French characters come alive by recitation of one of their famous passages, songs about them, or by students becoming the character through a dramatic presentation. Students could present in a musical dramatic fashion, complete with costume, the characters of Carmen (Bizet after Mérimée), Manon (Massenet after Prevost), Mignon (Thomas after Goethe), Melisande (Debussy after Maeterlinck) and others.

Often overlooked is the variety of French poetry set to music. Music settings are available for all eras, especially the nineteenth century. Poetry can be recited without music, but the music settings add another sense to the experience. Previous eras can be explored through poetry set to music in the twentieth century, like "Trois Ballades de Francois Villon" (Debussy), "Chansons de Ronsard" (Milhaud), or Villon's "Ballade des dames du temps jadis" set by Brassens. Many poems became popular songs in the twentieth century and are often familiar to Americans, such as "Feuilles mortes" ("Autumn Leaves").

Conclusion

A performance activity such as that suggested here adds a new dimension to language instruction, taking it beyond the familiar goals usually achieved within the classroom walls and encompassing the larger goals of culture and community addressed in the ACTFL standards. Extracurricular activities enhance traditional teaching by providing more depth and authenticity of linguistic practice and more opportunity for cultural exploration. Whereas many teachers have used songs in foreign language classes to reinforce grammatical structures and to teach culture, it is more relevant if students can put themselves into that role of King Louis XVI or the street urchin from Hugo's *Les Misérables*.

The chance to work with students in a different setting, seeing them outside of class, and participating with them on something creative within the subject area has many advantages. Since the teacher–student relationship works in a different manner, the teaching process still takes place, but without the formal setting of the classroom. The same concepts and cultural knowledge can be taught in a more relaxed atmosphere. Creating a mood in a certain historical situation for a stage performance is more comfortable than doing it in class. The extracurricular project described here lends itself to any language and culture, as each has its own unique elements. Most important is that students realize the importance of the foreign language itself and that it is a living language, not just one used in the classroom.

References

Abrate, Jayne. 1988. "Popular Music as a Foundation for a French Culture Course." *French Review* 62:217-41.

——. 1992. "The Popular Song: An Authentic Tool for Enriching the Foreign Language Classroom. *Creative Approaches in Foreign Language Teaching.*

Failoni, Judith. 1993. "Try Music!" *Visions and Reality in Foreign Language Teaching.* Report of Central States Conference on the Teaching of Foreign Languages.

Gardner, Howard. 1983. *Frames of Mind: The Theory of Multiple Intelligences.* New York: Basic Books.

——. 1993. *Multiple Intelligences: The Theory in Practice.* New York: Basic Books.

Hamblin, Vicki. 1987. "Integrating Popular Songs into the Curriculum." *French Review.* 60: 479-84.

Morain, Genelle. 1983. "Commitment to the Teaching of Foreign Cultures." *Modern Foreign Language Journal.* 67: iv.

Omaggio, Alice. 1986. *Teaching Language in Context.* Boston, Heinle & Heinle.

Theisen, Toni. 1997. "Exploring Multiple Intelligences: Respecting the Diversity of Learning." *Building Community Through Language Learning.* Report of Central States Conference on the Teaching of Foreign Languages.

Vialet, Michele. 1992. "L'Opéra en classe de français: du rock au baroque." *French Review.* 65: 589-601.

Appendix A (program)

Prelude - "Under Paris Skies" (instrumental with a slide show)

Pippin (Schwartz)

"War is a Science"

"Chevalier de la Table Ronde" (folk song)

La Révolution française (Boublil, Schonberg)

"Les Etats généraux:" Louis XVI, La Noblesse, Le Clergé, Le tiers etat

"Déclaration des droits de l'homme et du citoyen"

"You Went the Wrong Way Old King Louis" (American parody)

Candide (Bernstein)

"The Best of All Possible Worlds"

"Make Our Garden Grow"

"Frère Jacques" (folk song)

Les Misérables (Boublil, Schoenberg)

"At the End of the Day"

"I Dreamed a Dream"

"Do You Hear the People Sing?"

"On My Own"

"God on High"

"Finale"

Phantom of the Opera Medley (Lloyd Weber)

"Alouette" (folk song)

Can-Can (dance, music of Offenbach)

"Thank Heaven for Little Girls" (from *Gigi*)

"La Vie en rose" (Louiguy, Piaf)

"Milord" (Monnot, Moustaki)

"The Old Folks" (Brel)

"I Love Paris"

"La Marseillaise"

"If We Only Have Love" (Brel)

Appendix B (pretest and posttest)

Are you presently taking French?

How many years have you studied French?

Have you taken world history?

What is the capital of France?

Who was the great French conqueror of the Middle Ages?

Who was king just before the French Revolution?

Why was there a revolution in France?

What social classes were there during the revolution era?

What French author wrote *Candide?*

What French author wrote *Les Miserables?*

When does the action of *Les Miserables* take place?

What French author wrote *Phantom of the Opera?*

What is the song "Alouette" about?

Who was Edith Piaf?

Who was Jacques Brel?

What is the tone of much of the twentieth-century French popular music?

What is the name of the French national anthem?

Where and when did the can-can originate?

7
Music and Theater in the French Language Classroom
An Affective Bridge to Culture and Language

Sarah Gendron
Paige Gilbert
University of Wisconsin—Madison

Music and theater are wonderful ways to meld grammar and culture, while maintaining student interest. French teachers in the United States are often faced with university classrooms teeming with students who register for our classes simply in order to fulfill the foreign language requirement. Many departments do not seem bothered by this, content to simply fill their classes with warm bodies. Yet, once in the classroom students' lack of motivation and frustration can make teaching a formidable task. Without the possibility for immediate practical applications, students cannot help but perceive the second language as commercial and thus little more than yet one more "useless" but obligatory object of study. Given this situation, foreign language educators cannot simply teach grammatical rules and cafe vocabulary and hope that they will inspire in their students an appreciation for, and an understanding of, the French language and culture. The main problem with which we must contend is our geographical and affective distance from the target culture. It is this distance that breeds a lack of interest and renders a living language dead on its feet. In order to help students better understand the language that they are trying to learn, we must aid them to step outside of their own culture by introducing them to materials which allow them to understand a point of view that is different from their own.

The problem of cultural bias is one that can render difficult the process of learning a second/foreign language and is directly related to pragmatic failure.

Students transfer their cultural assumptions onto the target language, which causes conversational breakdown and misunderstandings. One of the ways to avoid these misunderstandings is to make students aware of what Claire Kramsch, among others, has called "cultural context". In her book, *Context and Culture in Language Teaching*, Kramsch (1993) describes how the underlying cultural assumptions that native speakers possess when they interact affect their discourse. She defines the term "context" to mean everything surrounding discourse:

> [Context is] not only spoken words, but facial expression, gestures, bodily activities, the whole group of people present during an exchange of utterances, and the part of the environment in which these people are engaged (Firth, cited by Kramsch 1993: 37).

Context thus plays a nonarticulated but central role in an exchange of utterances between native speakers. It is important to be aware of cultural context, for as Kramsch states:

> Native speakers of a language speak not only with their own individual voices, but through them speak also to the established knowledge of their native community and society, the stock of metaphors this community lives by, and the categories they use to represent their experience. (Kramsch 1993: 43)

Instructors can thus help bridge the gap by using authentic texts such as music and theater in the classroom, both as examples of "authentic language" and as a way to introduce various cultural points. One of the benefits of using music and theater in the classroom is that it is a way to teach students some of the cultural context of the second language culture, so that they can become aware of cultural references. This is especially true of popular music, which can give students insight into current musical tastes and cultural references. Both music and theater have many advantages over the use of other culturally relevant materials such as video clips, the Internet, or other realia. Besides the advantage of their limited length (which makes them ideal for the limits of the class period), both genres have the added advantage of being at once oral and textual, allowing the students to "live" the language in ways that would not otherwise be possible within the limits of the university classroom.

Although the use of music and theater in the foreign language classroom is not a new idea, much of what has been formally written in this area either does not speak to the needs of university-level students or is simply not practical within the limits of a fixed curriculum. Jayne Abrate's (1988) "Popular Music as a Foundation for a French Culture Course" offers an impressive comprehensive integration of music, slides, maps, and other realia to introduce students to French culture and language, but her method does not lend itself to instructors of beginning and intermediate-level language courses who are obliged to follow a specific curriculum. Our aim is thus to describe a number of ways in which varied genres of music and theater can be incorporated into a relatively fixed curriculum, in order to provide beginning- and intermediate-level undergraduates with a more direct link to the target culture than they would otherwise have had. All texts, both musical and dramatic, were chosen based on the cultural content they provide and according to their linguistic complexity, and most can be adapted for use in both beginning and intermediate levels.

Music: Creating an Affective Language Environment

One of the simplest ways to employ music in the foreign language classroom is to use it as "mood music." Playing any cassette from the target culture for five minutes before the class starts gives students the opportunity to affectively prepare themselves for the language before the class even begins. From the beginning of the semester, get in the habit of playing music as soon as students enter the classroom. While the music is playing and the instructor is in the process of setting up, have students find a partner with whom to spend a few minutes exchanging greetings in the target language. This warmup prepares the students mentally to learn French before the day's session ever begins. It is also a good idea to write the name of the artist, the title of the song, and the date it was recorded on the board. This is a good way to introduce the students to aspects of French culture to which they would not normally have access during the typical university semester. One possible way of organizing the music chosen is to do it chronologically, imparting on the student a sense of continuity and musical progression. The first month of class could be spent, for example, playing French music from the 1950s, and by the end of the semester they could be exposed to more contemporary music from the 1990s. It could also be arranged according to genre, beginning with classical music (a month divided among Debussy, Liszt, Poulenc, and Satie, for example), continuing with cabaret, then jazz, rock, pop, or whatever suits your personal interests.

This is also an ideal opportunity to introduce an aspect of francophone culture to the class. The use of music from a country other than France is often problematic due to the fact that much francophone music is not performed in French but rather in the language specific to that culture. The structure of "mood music" allows for its inclusion by not focusing specifically on language per se, but rather on the cultural aspect that it represents. The semester could be structured by spending one month on music from France, another from the Caribbean, followed by a month of French Canadian folk music, and finishing up with music from central and northern Africa.[1] At the more advanced levels this could be incorporated into a relatively structured yet personal "free-writing" exercise. Give the students an approximate page length that they will be expected to write (one paragraph) and an idea to focus on before the music has begun, such as asking them to concentrate on the images that the music stimulates or to imagine a scene where this type of music would play. This will provide them with enough guidance to successfully complete the task. After five to ten minutes of writing the students could then share their personal impressions with the class by reading their paragraph out loud.

Although the use of "mood music" is by far the simplest and least time-consuming way of bringing music into the foreign language classroom there are other ways that it can be used which have a more specific focus. For beginning-level undergraduate classes, the most popular is perhaps the use of music for its linguistic exploitation; to improve listening comprehension by exposing students to a wide range of voices and accents as well as to test their familiarity with particular grammatical structures. There are a number of ways that this type of activity can be employed, depending on the amount of time the instructor has available. If the focus is primarily that of listening comprehension, the instructor can prepare a brief exercise by simply removing particular grammatical elements (all possessive adjectives, nouns, or verbs of a particular tense) from the words of the song, depending on the particular grammar lesson. While most songs can be adapted to almost any grammatical focus, there are songs that lend themselves more easily to some grammar points than others. Céline Dion's "Pour que tu m'aimes encore" is, for example, a superb demonstration of the subjunctive in an authentic context. Edith Piaf's "La vie en rose," is, however, better suited for beginning students who are in the process of learning basic vocabulary and verbs in the present tense.[2] And Piaf's "Je ne regrette rien" works well as an exercise on negation.

After the desired elements have been removed from the text, the song is then played once while the students concentrate solely on general comprehension. The second time the song is played, they are instructed to fill in the missing elements. The third and last time that it is played is so that the students can check their work and fill in any words they missed the first time. The final check can be done either orally or by writing the answers on the board if spelling could be problematic.

A good way to expand this activity, if time permits, is to turn it into a pronunciation exercise. The most efficient way of accomplishing this is to give the students a limited number of rules to guide them in their reading. Tell students to cross out all unpronounced consonants, circle all [e] sounds and connect all liaisons in the text. After they have had a few minutes to mark their text, ask them to read one line at a time out loud until the entire text has been read. Once this task is completed, they will be ready (if not willing) to sing the song. Given that the students will most likely not be familiar with the tune and will not be as willing to participate without direct guidance, the most effective way to proceed is to sing each line and have them repeat immediately afterwards. In spite of the resistance that beginning students sometimes show when doing this activity for the first time, they often cite this as one of the most memorable activities performed in class.

For the more advanced intermediate-level students, the focus can be shifted from exclusively grammar to the cultural content of the music for the purpose of class discussions. After three semesters of French instruction many students are perfectly capable of presenting the material to the class on their own. This can be achieved through individual or small group research projects, where students are given time to explore and present some aspect of francophone culture to the class. As performance is an integral part of foreign language learning it is a good idea to encourage those that are interested in music to do research on a particular artist or genre and to present this information to the class, followed by a performance. One example of such a presentation from a first-year classroom was a brief talk on the origins of French Canadian folk music, after which the student sang a representative song to the class. Another example was a small group of students who presented a summary of the musical *Les Misérables*[3] and the historical period it represents, after which they led the class in singing one of the songs. Lyrics and sheet music as well as brief outlines of the project were prepared for the rest of the class in advance.

Popular music also works well to introduce different facets of French culture to students. One popular example is the music of French rapper MC Solaar, whose third album is currently a bestseller in Europe. Students find Solaar appealing because the music and lyrics are up to date. From an instructor's standpoint, Solaar's music is useful both for the way in which he plays with words and for the cultural details that he provides in his lyrics.

One example of a Solaar song that works well in the classroom is "Bouge de là," which is a great way to teach students about "verlan," a slang that is used by French youth. One suggestion for how to use the song in class is to have students read the words for homework or in class. Then give them a short lesson on "verlan" in which the syllables of words are reversed, creating the French equivalent of pig latin.[4] Then have students reread the text, circling all the "verlan" in the text. Then divide students into groups, and make each group responsible for explaining one stanza of the song. In this song, the narrator moves around Paris, encountering different people. Each group could then talk about the different people described in the song. After having discussed the text, have students listen to the song twice. The first time, have students list the various sounds (glass breaking, cars, etc.) that accompany each stanza. The second time, have students give an overall critique of the music. After having listened to the song, have students discuss their impressions of the music. You might also point out similarities and differences with American rap (i.e., not as violent, lots of bragging, etc.).

Francis Cabrel is another artist whose music works well in the classroom. In our second-year program, we have a unit on Provence in the south of France, in which we discuss bullfighting, or "la corrida," which is a popular tradition in southern French towns. One of the issues in this unit is a debate on whether or not bullfighting is cruel. To introduce this idea, Cabrel's song "La corrida" is particularly useful, because it personalizes the issue. "La corrida" is sung in the first person, and describes bullfighting from the point of view of the bull, and thus is a perfect lead-in to a discussion of tradition versus cruelty to animals. As with "Bouge de là," have students go over the text and put them in groups, assigning each group a stanza to prepare and discuss. Then have the students answer a series of questions about the cultural issues raised by the text, starting with comprehension questions and moving towards interpretation questions. For this section, ask them about the point of view of the narrator and the implied message of the song. At this point, play the song in class, and during this time, have students comment on the music. One aspect that comes up is the Spanish style used by Cabrel in this song. This leads easily into a discussion of the Spanish influence that pervades the culture of southern France.[5]

Another way to introduce students to music is to invite native speakers in the community to come to class to discuss music. For example, this week in a second-year French class, we invited a student from the Ivory Coast who is studying law at the University of Wisconsin. Rather than have him simply lecture about his country (which students tend to find dry) we asked him to play some music of his choice. He then went one step further and invited a friend who is a member of a dance troupe, and a student of traditional African music. So we were all treated to a performance of traditional African dance, in costume, which he finished by singing some of the traditional music of his country. The law student then explained in the target language the meaning behind the music and dance, which provided our students with a taste of the culture of the Ivory Coast. The student reaction was very positive—rather than simply listening to facts about a francophone country, they were able to learn a little about African culture through dance and music, while at the same time working on their French skills.

By incorporating culturally relevant materials that encourage active participation in the target language we can diminish the affective distance between the student learning the second language and the culture in which this language exists. The integration of theater and drama offer an additional rich resource for acquiring language and culture.

Theatrical Texts in the Classroom

While there are numerous ways one could employ theatrical texts in the foreign language classroom, two of the most efficient and effective are to use them as a listening comprehension activity or for role playing. One francophone playwright whose work can be easily adapted for use in beginning as well as intermediate-level French classes is Samuel Beckett. *En Attendant Godot* and *Oh les beaux jours,* both have the advantage of being linguistically simple texts that rely rather heavily on gestures for communication. As a listening comprehension exercise these both can work very well even in first semester French courses.

One possible way of presenting these texts is to choose a scene which the instructor and another colleague will act out in front of the class, having drawn the relevant scenery on the board. For the more advanced classes, two students could be chosen in advance to present the scene. In either case it is not necessary for those who are presenting the text to have it memorized. It is only important that the speech be smooth and natural and that the gestures coincide with the discourse.

The scene, which need be no longer than a few minutes, should be acted out two times. The first time, the students could be directed to listen and watch for general comprehension. After this has been acted out once, a sheet consisting of five to ten specific questions can be passed out to the class. The second time the scene is enacted, the students should then be instructed to listen and watch for the specific information listed.

In preparing the sheet of questions, it is not necessary that the questions be in French, especially at the beginning levels. What is important, however, is that the questions be in ascending order in terms of complexity. The first question would thus deal with more evident and concrete information, and the last would be more abstract, perhaps linking the text with the century in which it was written. Questions for a presentation of the hanging scene from *En Attendant Godot* could begin, for example, by calling attention to the scenery: Where does the scene take place? Would you characterize the scenery as sparse or excessive? The next few questions could emphasize the action: What are the three major actions that are performed in this scene? By what standard of measurement (height, weight, or intelligence) do the two characters decide who should be the first to hang himself? The final questions would then try to incorporate the above information to elicit a more abstract idea from the student: From what you have already discovered about the scene, can you deduce what the author is trying to say about human existence or the meaning of life? Is it possible to determine the century in which this play was written? How would you characterize the major social events in this century in comparison with the major events of the previous century? After the students have had a chance to think about the questions, five to ten minutes can then be spent in a general discussion of the scene.

Another way to employ authentic dramatic texts in class is to allow the students the opportunity to prepare and perform a text for the rest of the class. This works best as a small group activity, with two to four students per group. In the beginning level classes it is best to give each group the same text or short scene to work on. Perrault's "Le Petit chaperon rouge," can be easily adapted for this type of activity. For the intermediate level students, it might work better to assign a different scene of the same play to each group. Each scene would thus be presented in the order it appears in the text.

The most time effective way of integrating this activity is to assign the scene as homework to be read the night before. After having read the text students will be ready to work in small groups and prepare the scene. Putting a number of guidelines on the board can be very helpful for preparation. The students might be instructed, for example, to decide which students play the various roles and who will direct. Principal actions and necessary gestures could then be discussed. While beginning students will be obliged to rely on the text when performing their scene, more advanced students should be directed to reformulate the necessary dialogue in their own words. This preparation need not take any more than ten minutes of class time. Once the students have had the time to rehearse, each group can then be called upon to perform its scene before the class. Each presentation can then be followed by a general discussion as to the effectiveness of the group's personal interpretation.

Using theater in the foreign language classroom need not be limited, however, to the employment of dramatic texts. Drama techniques are in themselves a valuable resource in the second language classroom. Patricia Dickson's (1989) "Acting French: Drama Techniques in the Second Language" is a comprehensive presentation of the various ways in which improvisation and dramatic monologues can help beginning- and intermediate-level students become more proficient in the target language. According to Dickson, with the exception of complete immersion, there is no better way to achieve linguistic and affective acquisition of a second language than through the use of drama techniques. Both acting and learning a second language focus not only on self-expression through speech patterns, but also on communicating meaning through the use of physical gestures. Language teaching should thus not be limited to exercising the mind and the vocal cords, but expanded to include the body.

The examples Dickson (1989) gives for the use of such techniques in the classroom range from vocal and physical warm-up exercises to the acting out of improvisational scenes based on the daily vocabulary. While the activities she suggests are "authentic" in the sense that they are unscripted, as is communication in daily life, they allow for very little cultural exposure. To remedy this dilemma, one could apply drama techniques to diverse forms of literature, by making the nontheatrical texts theatrical.

There are many different ways this type of technique could be integrated in·the intermediate-level lesson plan. If the instructor is particularly pressed for time, shorter texts such as fables or poetry would work best. One could take, for example, four or five of La Fontaine's fables and assign each small group of three to four students one fable to prepare and present to the class. Limiting the preparation time to five to ten minutes can help to speed up the process. Some general guidelines, such as deciding who will play which parts, and which particular actions must be represented, should also be given in advance. Any necessary dialogue should be reformulated in the student's own words. After the ten minutes of preparation, each group can then present their fable to the class. The rest of the class could perhaps then try to come up with the moral.

Literary texts often present a challenge to first- and second-year students. For this reason, having students stage excerpts from the text can really help them to understand the subtleties of both the target language in the text and the themes that the author is trying to convey. Another literary genre that lends itself well to dramatization is poetry. By dramatizing poems in class, instructors can help students to hear the beauty of the poetic language, while at the same time helping them understand themes and vocabulary that could pose a problem otherwise. Two poems that work well in class are "Déjeuner du matin" by Prévert and "Le Pain" by Ponge. Prévert's poetry works well because it is easy to understand and it often tells a story. Some of his poetry is even in the form of a dialogue. For this reason, it can be used in both first- and second-year classrooms. "Déjeuner du matin" is a poem in which a woman describes the indifference of her husband by describing the way in which he ignores her during breakfast. There are thus two characters at a breakfast table and students can act out each action of the breakfast while they recite the poem. The poem is written in the past tense, so students can reinforce an important grammatical point as well as their pronunciation. A follow-up activity might be to have students restate the action of the poem in prose form, or have them write a one paragraph resume of the action. Then they could discuss the themes of the poem.

Dramatization can also help students to visualize texts that are particularly challenging. In our second-year program, we do a unit organized around the theme of the importance of bread in French culture. For this unit, students read a poem called "Le Pain" by Ponge. Ponge is a twentieth-century poet who writes poetry based on objects taken from everyday life. His technique is to make familiar objects appear unfamiliar, so that they seem strange. Because of this, his poems sometimes resemble riddles, in which it is hard to recognize the object intended. Dramatization helps students to visualize the metaphors in the text. For this poem, we start off by going over some of the vocabulary associated with bread. We then brainstorm some possible metaphors for bread, which one of the students writes on the board. We then place students in a circle and give them each a portion of a baguette. Then, we go around the room and have students read the poem to see how Ponge arrived at his metaphors. In the poem, Ponge describes the bread as if it were a mountain, and then as if it were under a microscope. By reading the poem together while looking at the bread, students have a much better sense of what Ponge is trying to do in the poem.

Excerpts from texts can also be dramatized in class, to aid students not only with vocabulary and pronunciation, but with the visualization of the scene. Staging these scenes also helps students to see the different ways in which the same scene can be interpreted differently, which helps them to see the particular point of view stressed by the author. For example, in our second-year program, students read excerpts from Emile Zola's novel *Germinal*. This text, set in the north of France in the nineteenth century, describes the struggle and poverty of the coal miners, versus the wealth and privilege of the upper-middle-class owners of the mine. The excerpts that we use in class focus on a family of coal miners and the family that operates the mine. This text works well for second-year students because the contrasts between the Maheu and the Grégoire are sharply drawn, and it is relatively easy for them to compare and contrast the two families. However, the texts do contain difficult vocabulary, which is one advantage of having students dramatize them in class. For this exercise, we divide our students into three groups—one group for each scene. Although all the students have read the three scenes, we make each group responsible for staging one scene and for explaining their scene to the class. We then provide them with a list of characters from the scene. It is their responsibility to assign roles, create dialogue (drawing from the text) and make decisions regarding staging, props, costumes and lighting. The students must also decide whether they will use a narrator to read Zola's text or have different characters provide scenic details. Our only instructions are that everyone have a speaking role and that they stick as close to the text as possible. We usually give them some time in class to work on this, and then they are responsible for meeting outside of class to rehearse briefly. On presentation day, students stage their scenes and engage in a general discussion about the various interpretations of the scenes and the choices that students made in staging them. We usually find that students have a lot to say about their particular scene and the dramatic choices that they made. We then watch the same scenes as interpreted by Claude Berri in the film version of *Germinal*. Having staged the scenes themselves, students are eager to critique the film for differences with the text, such as the glamorization of the miners in the film.

Staging scenes from *Germinal* thus allows students to work on several skills. By summarizing the text and creating dialogue, the students work on vocabulary and reading comprehension. The students then work on their oral skills by staging the scene. Most importantly, a better understanding of what is being read is gained by acting it out. Analytical skills are emphasized as students are asked to compare their choices with those made by the director of the film version of *Germinal*.

Conclusion

As instructors, one of the most important lessons we can give our students is to help them step outside their own culture to be able to appreciate the world that surrounds them. Students are often under the impression that the second language that they are learning exists in a vacuum, with no real relevance to their daily lives. One of the ways to bridge the gap between cultures that seems to be endemic to the second language classroom is to import cultural documents that allow them access to the established knowledge of the second language community. Music and theater are excellent examples of authentic texts and "living language" that can be used both to demonstrate various cultural points and to allow students to see the target language in an appropriate context. As explored in this article, there are many ways in which to incorporate both music and theater into a fixed curriculum. Music can be used to create a mood, for example, or to illustrate a point of grammar. Dramatic presentations can help students to understand difficult literary texts and to participate actively in their own learning. It is for this reason that music and theater can be used both to maintain student interest in the language, and overcome the barriers caused by their affective and geographical isolation from the target culture.

Notes

1. Most of this music can be found in international sections of local music stores, but if you are looking for a specific artist there are distributors on the Internet who take special orders.
2. The lyrics to these songs and countless others can be obtained by way of the Internet using the Alta Vista or Yahoo search engine (French version) followed by a search using the artist's name.
3. Lyrics for every song from this musical can also be found through the Internet using the Alta Vista search engine. The compact disc can be found at almost any music store.
4. David Burke (1995) gives an explanation of "verlan" in his book *Street French,* published by John Wiley and Sons, Inc.
5. Another way to work music into a discussion of the south of France is to show the bullfighting scene from the recent French film version of Bizet's *Carmen,* starring Placido Domingo. This provides students with a visual representation of bullfighting, while at the same time exposing them to some great opera music in French.

References

Abrate, Jayne. 1988. "Popular Music as a Foundation for a French Culture Course." *The French Review* 62, 2.

Burke, David. 1995. *Street French*. New York; John Wiley and Sons.

Dickson, Patricia S. 1989. "Acting French: Drama Techniques in the Second Language Classroom." *The French Review* 63, 2.

Kramsch, Claire.1993. *Context and Culture in Language Teaching*. New York: Oxford University Press.

Appendix

List of Suggested Songs and Texts

Songs:

Dion, Céline. "Pour que tu m'aimes encore." *The French Album*. Song Music, 1994.

Cabrel, Françis. "La corrida." *Samedi soir sur la terre,* 1994.

Piaf, Edith. "La Vie en Rose." *Disque d'or.* EMI.

Solaar, M.C. "Paradisiaque." *Paradisiaque* Paris: Polydor, 1997.

Literary Texts:

Beckett, Samuel. *En Attendant Godot*. New York: Macmillan, 1963.

————. "Oh les beaux jours." Paris: Les Editions de minuit, 1963.

Colette. "L'Autre femme." *La femme cachée*. Paris: Flammarion, 1995.

La Fontaine. *Fables de La Fontaine*. Paris: Librairie de L. Hachette, 1898.

Perrault, Charles. "Le petit chaperon rouge." *Les Contes de Perrault*. Paris: Sacelp, 1980.

Prévert, Jacques. *Paroles*. Paris: Editions Gallimard, 1949.

Zola, Emile. *Germinal*. New York: E.P. Dutton, 1952.

8
Pop Culture and the Three C's

Joan Turner
Heather Mendoza
University of Arkansas—Fayetteville

The T-shirt with its inevitable message gracing both front and back sides reflects to a surprising degree the popular thought of a culture. One of the latest T-shirt slogans states "Been there . . . done that" which often seems to be the message teachers receive from their students in 3rd and 4th year high school language classes. From the teacher's point of view, these classes should be the most rewarding for students because they can finally express themselves in a coherent way in the target language. From the student point of view, the classroom experience is often another dose of more of the same. These jaded students, however, will shed their bored expressions when they participate in school dances, sporting events, and even after-school jobs. The challenge of the language teacher is to discover a way to channel this energy and enthusiasm into the classroom setting.

The question of how to motivate students is certainly not a new one. Early research by Gardner and Lambert (1972) divides the concept of motivation into two categories: instrumental motivation, the motivation to learn a language in order to achieve a goal such as getting a job, translating a work, or even getting a good grade; and integrative motivation, the motivation that stems from a positive feeling toward the speakers of a language and their culture and a desire to become a part of it. The two types of motivation are not mutually exclusive and most learners experience a mixture of both. Nevertheless, to the teacher facing an intermediate class on a Monday morning, both types of motivation seem to exist on a higher plane than what is readily apparent in the classroom.

More recent research has begun to recognize that the foreign language learning situation consists of still other variables. Crookes and Schmidt (1991) propose four conditions for motivation: interest, relevance, expectancy, and satisfaction. Based on findings from the research of educational psychology,

104

Dornyei (1994) suggests a series of ways to motivate students in the language class: increase the attractiveness of the course content by using authentic materials that are within the students' grasp; utilize unusual and exotic supplementary materials, recordings, and visual aids; arouse and sustain curiosity and attention by introducing unexpected, novel, unfamiliar, and even paradoxical events; increase students' interest and involvement in the tasks by designing or selecting varied and challenging activities; adapt tasks to the students' interest; make sure that something about each activity is new or different; increase student expectancy of task fulfillment by familiarizing students with the task type; and facilitate student satisfaction by allowing students to create finished products. These recommendations for student motivation appear to be rather daunting at first glance when the teacher has not even begun to deal with the curricular demands of the language teaching situation.

The authors have attempted to bridge the gap between student satisfaction and teacher goals by producing a model that is based on an aspect of pop culture and is guided by the principles of cognitive psychology, content-enriched instruction, and communicative language teaching. An aspect of pop culture serves as the content of the model because students are more apt to be motivated by figures and events that they are already acquainted with through radio, television, and magazines. The role of content in this model is to promote active participation in language learning by providing students with a vehicle for communication. The goals of this unit reflect the following National Standards (Lafayette 1996) for communication:

1.1 Students engage in conversations, provide and obtain information, express feelings and emotions, and exchange opinions.

1.2 Students understand and interpret written and spoken language on a variety of topics.

1.3 Students present information, concepts, and ideas to an audience of listeners or readers on a variety of topics.

The unit does not impose the acquisition of specific grammar structures as goals. Instead, we have suggested grammar points that might be most appropriate given the materials based on *Evita*. Thus, it is possible for each teacher to focus on particular grammar structures according to the needs of his or her students.

POP CULTURE

Cognitive Principles

Content Enrichment

Communication

Figure 1. Pop culture model

Cognitive Theory

The success or failure of many activities conducted by foreign language teachers can be traced back to certain principles of cognitive psychology. Whether representing the brain as a type of filing cabinet or as a computer, cognitive psychologists believe that knowledge is organized and represented in memory by means of interconnected propositions or statements. When the individual recalls information, these propositional networks are translated into familiar verbal and pictorial codes. Ausubel, Novak, and Hanesian (1968) were early proponents of applying the principles of cognitive psychology to verbal learning. They define the concept of "cognitive structure" as the quantity, clarity, and organization of the learner's present knowledge in a particular subject area. The knowledge, consisting of facts, concepts, and raw data, is arranged in a hierarchical manner. New information can be related to the existing structure but may require the rearrangement of the system. Ausubel et al. (1968) propose that meaningful material can be assimilated if it is related to what the learner already possesses in the cognitive structure. Craik and Lockhart (1972) add that the more links there are between new and previously learned knowledge, the greater the depth of processing and the stronger the memory link.

Ausubel et al. (1968) also stress the importance of advance organizers or techniques to activate relevant preexisting or background knowledge. Advance organizers are general ideas that give the student an overview of what is to be learned and thus provide linkage to the cognitive structure. There are several advantages to their use: (1) they draw upon relevant anchoring concepts already in the student's cognitive structure and allow for the new material to be assimilated; (2) they allow the assimilated new material to serve as an anchor for future knowledge; and (3) they enhance meaningfulness and diminish the student's need to learn terms through rote memory.

Rumelhart (1980) and other proponents of schema theory hold that all knowledge is packaged into units or schemata. Comprehension is an interactive process that occurs between the learner with his background knowledge and the text, whether it be oral or written. Unless the learner has the appropriate background knowledge or schema, comprehension will not occur. According to Lee and VanPatten (1995) schemata serve to decrease ambiguity in the text, elaborate on elements of information, provide a perspective on the information in the text, and compensate for missing knowledge. This personal knowledge must be activated, however, to maximize comprehension. The degree of learning that follows is also dependent on how much linkage has occurred. In addition, retrieval of this information will be affected by the number of mutual connections.

Schema theory has been used by foreign language educators to account for differences in learning among students. Storme and Siskin (1989) stress the role of background knowledge in reading comprehension, specifically linguistic knowledge such as lexical meaning, word derivation, syntactic rules, and verb tenses as well as the reader's knowledge of the world. According to Omaggio (1993) both reading and listening comprehension require the same type of background preparation and at lower levels of proficiency, extra-linguistic cues and advance organizers can activate schemata in order to compensate for gaps in comprehension created by an incomplete knowledge of the linguistic code.

Content Enrichment

For some time foreign language educators have recommended that language be taught not in isolated units but within a meaningful context. The richness of the context should aid the learner in making connections based on meaning, which in turn allows for new material to be attached to the cognitive structure. Authentic texts allow the vocabulary and structure to be taught in a natural setting. The popularity of content-based approaches can be traced to the desire to reduce the artificial separation of language teaching and subject matter. Krahnke (1987) contends that students who are not motivated to participate in a class whose main focus is linguistic may be willing to practice language when it is used as a vehicle to deliver interesting content. In such approaches, activities are based on the subject matter being taught but are still connected to the framework of listening, speaking, reading, and writing.

Brinton, Snow, and Bingham Wesche (1989) present a further rationale for the teaching of language and content. They state that for language learning to occur, the language syllabus must take into account the learner's needs and the use that s/he will make of the target language. The use of content that is perceived by the learner as relevant should lead to increased motivation, greater willingness to practice, and more effective learning. Content-based approaches often tend to build on the learner's existing knowledge of the subject matter as well as the new linguistic knowledge to be assimilated. They further recommend that language be taught through a focus on contextualized use rather than through isolated samples of correct usage. Finally, they reiterate Krashen's (1982) view that the input must be understood by the learner and that the learner can benefit not only from situational and verbal contexts but also from his/her knowledge of the world. A content-based approach with its blending of form and meaning necessary for comprehension enables the learner to add to a developing network of lexical and semantic relationships.

Leaver and Stryker (1989) trace the development of content-based instruction to the 1980s with its emphasis on communicative competence. Nevertheless, content-based instruction was evident in Canada in the 1960s in the form of immersion programs which came to the attention of foreign language educators everywhere. Content-based instruction has received recognition not only in Canada but in ESL and FLES programs in the United States. At the university level, content-based instruction occurs in courses described as language across the curriculum and language for special purposes.

Brinton et al. (1989) describe three models of content-based instruction to be found at the university level: sheltered courses, which consist of content courses taught in the target language by a content specialist who is also fluent in that language; adjunct language instruction in which students are enrolled in two linked courses: a content course and a language course whose topics and assignments are linked; and theme-based language instruction in which the content presented provides the basis for language analysis and practice. The third option is most appropriate for the model to be presented. In such an approach, a reading selection might be provided as background knowledge with vocabulary supplied to aid in later discussions for speaking practice. Video or audio tapes would provide listening comprehension and writing assignments would be used for rounding out the unit. This approach differs from the more traditional course where these activities exist in isolation and seldom center around a given theme.

The topic-based approach can comprise an entire course or just one unit depending on the setting, the curriculum, and the proficiency of the students. Ballman (1997) advocates the use of a topic-based approach even at the elementary level and refers to such teaching as content-enriched instruction. She adds that language learning will be enhanced if from the beginning students are exposed to a language curriculum that integrates cultural and real world information. According to Mohan (1986) activities in a content-based course can be divided into expository approaches and experiential approaches. In an expository approach, activities might consist of listening to lectures, reading articles, or classroom discussions while in an experiential approach students perform role plays and simulations, attend demonstrations, interview native speakers, or participate in field trips. These activities typically occur in a language class based on a communicative approach.

Communicative Language Teaching

Ausubel's et al. (1968) work in the 1960s did much to promote the learning of language in a meaningful context, a marked contrast to the rote learning that had gone on before. In the next decade, further attention was given to developing a communicative approach that focused on the learner rather than the teacher and on language in natural conversation rather than in pattern drills or memorized dialogues. Savignon (1983) advocates a communicative approach that is based on topics that appeal to the learner, a functional treatment of grammar, and attention paid to content rather than merely accuracy. The affective needs of the student are addressed as students begin to speak about their own lives and those of their fellow students.

Classroom activities were also affected by the communicative approach and whole class instruction was now interspersed with small group or pair activity. Some of the more popular activities for small group work include the following:

1. Think-pair-share (Kagan 1989) in which students listen to a question posed by the teacher, consider a possible answer, discuss that answer with a partner, and then share their response with the whole group;

2. Jig-saw puzzle (Kagan 1989) in which each member of a group has been given a unique portion of information which s/he must share with the entire group in order to solve a problem;

3. Information gap (Johnson 1979) in which one student has information that another student does not have but needs in order to complete his/her part of an activity; and

4. Movement activities (Bassano and Christison 1987) in which the student must survey the other members of the class for their responses to a particular question.

Other popular communicative activities take the form of role-plays, debates, problem solving, and simulations.

The Pop Culture Model

The pop culture model reflects each of the components mentioned above. The need to motivate students is of prime concern in any teaching situation. This is especially true in the third and fourth years of language teaching, where the novelty of beginning a language has worn off. Students are faced with a significant corpus of vocabulary and grammar structures that must be recycled and yet combined with new material. Students have already had practice in describing their families, friends, schools, and the activities of their daily lives. The idea for the unit described below occurred when one of the authors was seated in a movie theater awaiting the start of the film *Evita*. The theater was filled not with adults interested in some facet of the history of Argentina or a reproduction of a Broadway play, but rather with a group of excited teenagers eager to see Madonna and Antonio Banderas. When the movie began, the teenagers quietly watched the unraveling of a drama with a historical basis. The content of the drama is interesting to students because it takes place in this century, reflects a coming-of-age theme, and contains a historical background that can be emphasized according to the interests and level of the students.

Sample Teaching Unit

Often the course of pop culture is directed by what is publicized by the media. The recent popularity of the movie *Evita* makes the life of Eva Perón a motivating theme for students. Of course, this is but one example of a possible unit theme taken from pop culture. As the popularity of *Evita* fades, the

Spanish teacher must look for other sources that can be adapted to the classroom. The topic chosen may be adapted from a popular song, dance, event, or public figure. Recent examples of such items include the movie *Selena,* the *Macarena* dance, TV personality Daisy Fuentes, or baseball star Fernando Valenzuela.

The authors have designed a sample teaching unit based on the life of Evita which was an element of pop culture when the unit was designed. The unit presents activities based on three media in the following order: film, music, and print. The order in which the media are presented, however, is not necessarily sequential. Instructors may opt, for example, to use a reading as an advance organizer rather than a video. Several variations are possible; the authors demonstrate only one of these.

In most cases if the pop culture item has been widely publicized there will be one or more videos available that can be used in the classroom. For the sample teaching unit, the video chosen by the authors is a biographical special[1] about the life of Eva Perón rather than the movie *Evita* that many of the students will have already seen in theaters. The movie *Evita* may also serve as an advance organizer. The authors chose a nonfiction version in order to provide the students with a historical yet interesting overview.

Film

A video about a historical figure such as Eva Perón lends itself to a variety of activities. In order to insure that the discussion of questions in activities will be done in the target language rather than in English, it will be necessary to insure that all students begin with the same knowledge base by providing students with a list of appropriate vocabulary. Because material on historical figures tends to be biographical, narrating the events of a lifetime, it is particularly well adapted for use with the preterite versus the imperfect, descriptive adjectives, dates and numbers, and the subjunctive (impersonal expressions, hypothetical situations, adverbial clauses, etc.). Rather than teaching these grammar points separately, the instructor should incorporate them into content-enriched activities in order to provide a context for the exercises. Students may, for example, be given a handout narrating a scene from a video they have watched. They then fill in the blanks with either the preterite or imperfect form of the verb given.

The authors begin the unit with the presentation of a video in English as an advance organizer that provides the students with an overall view of what they will be learning. Before showing the film, it is helpful to have the students answer questions (true/false, multiple choice, etc.) and discuss what they already know or think about the *Evita* theme in order to relate it to their own life experience, which forms the basis of their cognitive structures. This activity can even be done as a survey with students circulating around the room to question their classmates. Later, the members of the class can discuss their findings. It is also a good idea to give the students questions to answer while watching the video in order to focus their attention. Questions requiring long answers should probably be avoided, however, so that students will not miss key points while giving lengthy answers.

After viewing the film, the instructor can assign think-pair-share activities having students discuss their responses to questions such as:

1. Would you have the story end differently, and if so how?
2. Who would you cast as actors if you were directing the production?
3. Which characters do you identify with most and why?
4. Do you know anyone like these characters?
5. Do the characters seem real to you?

As with all pair activities, the instructor would also compare answers of the class as a whole.

Several other activities could be designed using a timeline based on events presented in the video as a contextual framework . One such activity involves giving each member of the class a list of main events that are arranged randomly so that students can work in pairs or small groups to put them in the correct order. The arrangement of events could also be utilized as a jigsaw activity in which each class member is given an event and then must form a human "timeline" along with his/her classmates in accordance with the sequence of events. A timeline could also be used as the basis of an information gap activity in which students are given two different versions of the timeline. They then work in pairs trying to fill in the gaps in their own version of the timeline by asking questions about their partner's version and vice-versa. In order to conclude the video portion of the unit, students may repeat the survey they took before watching the video and compare the results with the information they collected previously.

Music

Pop culture themes may also be developed through the use of songs currently popular among students. In this unit, based on the life of Evita, it is likely that students are already familiar with the English version of the song, *Don't Cry For Me Argentina*.[2] Therefore, the instructor might begin by having students discuss their reactions to the lyrics in order to activate their background knowledge. For example, can students identify with the emotions or situation presented by the song? Next, students decide where along the timeline they will place the song in accordance with the other events in Evita's life. Because the authors were able to find both the Spanish and the English versions of the theme song from *Evita,* they created activities in which students compare and contrast the two versions. The Spanish version[3] alone may be used as an exercise in listening comprehension by giving the lyrics to the students with blanks to be filled in as they listen. Songs whose lyrics are written in the target language may also be used for pronunciation practice by having the class sing the song. In addition, students may draw a picture based on the song and then share their interpretation with the class; or students could work in groups, each group drawing pictures of the images from one stanza to be later shared with the group as a whole. As teaching material the song also lends itself to an analysis of literary devices such as imagery, word play, similes, and metaphors. Thus, the instructor may also choose to utilize methods appropriate for the teaching of poetry. As a final song activity, learners can work in groups to add a stanza of their own to the song.

Print

Pop culture may also be introduced into the classroom through print. Reading materials reflecting aspects of pop culture may be obtained from a wide variety of sources. Instructors can create materials if necessary, however, authentic materials are recommended. Sources of authentic readings include: books, magazine articles, short stories, selections from personal journals, letters, newspaper articles, advertisements, etc. Readings may be written in English or in the target language depending on the pedagogical goals of the instructor. A general background reading written in English can be assigned to the students when starting the unit in order to insure that all begin with the same knowledge framework. Later in the unit, it may also be appropriate to include shorter readings written in the target language. The authors chose a short children's reader[4] in Spanish because of its simple language structure and detailed illustrations. This short reading in the target language lends itself to several communicative activities allowing students to interact with the material in a creative way. The instructor may introduce the learners to the reading by separating the text from the illustrations and asking them to describe the people in the drawings. When students complete the reading they may look at the drawings again and see how closely their own descriptions match the content of the story. If a text is not illustrated the students can create a content map[5] after reading the assignment. This activity helps students understand the story by reducing the plot to its main events. Students, individually or in small groups, make a list of the most important actions of the story once again relating elements in the students' existing cognitive structures with the new material being presented. Next, they briefly depict each scene and arrange their drawings in chronological order. In order to help students better visualize the text, members of the class may also choose a scene from the text and present it as a skit or short play. This activity may conclude by having the 'audience' discuss some of the ideas they saw presented. The instructor may end this section of the unit with a class discussion of how the reading confirmed or contradicted the information collected in the survey taken both before and after viewing the video.

Culminating Activities

In order to help students assimilate the material presented in the unit, the authors have designed several culminating activities. These activities include the production skills of speaking and writing and enable learners to bring together the content and linguistic structures that are presented throughout the unit. The instructor may choose from the following activities.

Students may develop their ideas about the pop culture theme through the use of creative writing assignments. This type of activity can be used to cover a variety of different grammar points depending on the teacher's goals for the unit. In one activity students write an entry in Evita's diary based on an assigned event from the timeline mentioned previously. Upon completing the assignment students read their compositions aloud while their classmates attempt to guess which event they are describing. Other assignments may include writing Evita's obituary or a newspaper article describing one of the events from her life. In addition, students may write an essay in which they consider the general theme and apply it to their own experience. Students may, for example, develop a comparison between Eva Perón and women who have recently held important public positions, such as the late Princess Diana or Hillary Clinton. As a class the students then categorize similarities and differences on the chalkboard. Next, each student writes a composition comparing these famous women.

Speaking activities may take the form of debates, oral presentations, and simulations. One activity requires that the students debate whether or not Evita should be characterized as "sinner" or "saint." Students may also practice communicating in the target language by working in pairs or small groups to describe the people and events shown in actual photos found in biographical texts. In addition, learners can participate in simulations in which each member of the class assumes the role of an individual who had contact with Evita (i.e., sister, husband, Argentinean worker, etc.). Through the use of such culminating activities, students are able to reflect on the main aspects of the unit thus providing greater linkage within the students' cognitive structures.

Conclusion

The story behind the Evita theme allows for ample practice of structures and vocabulary in a contextualized setting. That the movie begins with the young Eva Perón makes it easier for students to identify on an affective level with such elements as the death of a parent, the drive to gain recognition, and the belief that success and excitement lie in the city. The use of multiple modalities—music, film, and print—appeal to individual learning styles of the students. As in any communicative activity, the success of the unit depends on the pre-preparation or activities that access the schemata in the student's cognitive structure. With this unit, the authors have attempted to provide a method for motivating students while increasing their linguistic capabilities and heightening their cultural awareness.

Notes

1. Several biographical videos based on the life of Eva Perón are available, such as those produced by A&E, PBS, or Lifetime Entertainment.
2. The authors chose the version sung by Madonna on the original soundtrack of the motion picture *Evita* (Warner Bros. 1996).
3. Various recordings of "No llores por mi Argentina" may be ordered through bookstores. The authors chose to use Paloma San Basilio's recording of the song contained on the album entitled *Mis mejores canciones: 17 super éxitos* (Capitol 1993).
4. The authors chose *Evita* by Hugh Probyn (Harrap 1977) as the reading selection on which to base their activities.
5. For a more detailed explanation of content mapping see Turner and Cowell (1996, pp. 225-26).

References

Ausubel, David P., Novak, Joseph D., and Hanesian, Helen. 1968. *Educational Psychology: A Cognitive View*. New York: Holt, Rinehart and Winston.

Ballman, Terry L. 1997. "Enhancing Beginning Language Courses Through Content-Enriched Instruction." *Foreign Language Annals* 30, 2:173-186.

Bassano S., and Christison, M. A. 1987. "Developing Successful Conversation Groups." Eds. M.H. Long and J. C. Richards. *Methodology in TESOL: A Book of Readings*. New York: Newbury House.

Brinton, Donna M., Snow, Marguerite Ann, and Bingham Wesche, Marjorie. 1989. *Content-Based Second Language Instruction*. New York: Newbury House.

Craik, Fergus I. M., and Lockhart, Robert. 1972. "Levels of Processing: A Framework for Memory Research." *Journal of Verbal Learning and Verbal Behavior* 11: 671-84.

Crookes, Graham and Schmidt. 1991. Motivation: Reopening the Research Agenda. *Language Learning* 41: 469-512.

Dornyei, Zoltán.1994. "Motivation and Motivating in the Foreign Language Classroom." *Modern Language Journal* 78, iii: 273-284.

Gardner, Robert, and Lambert, Wallace E. 1972. *Attitudes and Motivation in Second Language Learning*. Rowley, MA: Newbury House Publishers.

Johnson, K. 1979. Communicative Approaches and Communicative Processes. Eds. C. J. Brunfit and K. Johnson. *The Communicative Approach to Language Teaching*. Oxford: Oxford University Press.

Kagan, S. 1989. *Cooperative Learning Resources for Teachers*. San Juan Capistrano, CA: Resources for Teachers.

Krahnke, Karl. 1987. *Approaches to Syllabus Design for Foreign Language Teaching*. Englewood Cliffs, NJ: Prentice Hall.

Krashen, S. 1982. *Principles and Practice in Second Language Acquisition*. New York: Pergamon Press.

Lafayette, Robert C., ed. 1996. *National Standards: A Catalyst for Reform*. Lincolnwood, IL: National Textbook, 211-212.

Leaver, Betty Lou, and Stryker, Stephen B. 1989. "Content-Based Instruction for Foreign Language Classrooms." *Foreign Language Annals* 22, 3: 269-275.

Lee, James F., and VanPatten, Bill. 1995. *Making Communicative Language Teaching Happen*. New York: McGraw Hill.

Mohan, Bernard A. 1986. *Language and Content*. Reading, MA: Addison-Wesley.

Omaggio Hadley, Alice. 1993. *Language Teaching in Context*. Boston, MA: Heinle & Heinle.

Rumelhart, D. 1980. Schemata: The Building Blocks of Cognition. In R. Sprio, B. Bruce & W. Brewer (Eds.) *Theoretical Issues in Reading Comprehension*. Hillsdale. NJ: Lawrence Erlbaum.

Savignon, S. 1983. *Communicative Competence: Theory and Practice*. Reading, MA: Addison-Wesley.

Storme, Julie A., and Siskin, H. Jay. 1989. "Developing Extensive Reading Skills: The Transition to Literature." In *Defining the Essentials for the Foreign Language Classroom,* David McAlpine (Ed.) Lincolnwood, IL: National Textbook.

Turner, Joan F., and Cowell, Glynis. 1996. A Cognitive Model for the Teaching of the Literary Elements. In *Patterns and Policies: The Changing Demographics of Foreign Language Instruction,* Judith E. Liskin-Gasparro, ed. Boston: Heinle & Heinle, 213-229.

9
Multiculturalism Across the German Curriculum
The Michigan State Model

Thomas Lovik
Patrick McConeghy
Elizabeth Mittman
Patrick Paulsell
George Peters
Michigan State University

Introduction

Issues of diversity and multiculturalism have been high on the agenda of the American Association of Teachers of German for nearly ten years now, since the formation, in 1988, of a special task force for minority recruitment and retention in German. Sessions devoted to the topic have been held at every national meeting of the AATG since then. The association's committee on minorities in German has produced a diversity of resource materials for national distribution. A special issue of the association's pedagogical journal, *Die Unterrichtspraxis–Teaching German,* focused on diversity (25.2, 1992). The dismal statistics in the last AATG membership survey recording minority participation in both the teaching and learning of German in the U.S. helped spur committed teachers around the country into action (Schulz, 1993).

It is difficult to assess exactly what has been accomplished. Both published and anecdotal evidence suggests that there has been progress, that more teachers are including more units on diversity and multiculturalism in their German curricula than before. Texts written by foreigners living in Germany, units on the Holocaust and on the White Rose resistance movement, discussion of *Ausländerfeindlichkeit* (xenophobia) and the political debate on *Asylanten* (asylum seekers) in Germany—these are but a few examples of topics that are commonly treated in both high school and university German classes.

In 1992, when the entire curriculum at Michigan State University (MSU) had to be revised due to the transition from quarters to semesters, the German faculty decided that issues of diversity and multiculturalism in the context of German Studies should be integrated into the curriculum at every level, ideally into every course. Although the decision was influenced by the national agenda set by the AATG, the faculty was primarily motivated by a perception that modern Germany is, in fact, rapidly becoming a multicultural society—whether it wants to be or not—and that an understanding of Germany today, which is one of the stated objectives of the German major at MSU, cannot be complete without attention to this crucial aspect of German culture and society. It is a complex and controversial topic, one that cannot adequately be treated in an isolated course or in disparate units scattered throughout the curriculum. The attempt in the program at MSU is to include discussion of the various issues relating to the presence of ethnic minorities in Germany—from historical perspectives, to social and political realities, to cultural manifestations—at every stage of a student's progress through the program. The purpose of this article is to convey accurately how this works in practice and to illustrate how individual instructors at each level of the undergraduate program attempt to realize this goal.

If the profession is to make significant strides in attracting more minority students to the study of German, German teachers must make a concerted effort to portray contemporary Germany as a country that is far more foreigner friendly and racially tolerant than is generally supposed. This is not to suggest that problems be surpressed, nor that the racial hatred and insensitivity that still exist in Germany be ignored. The attempt must be to include in American students' study of German language and culture an accurate and honest portrayal of how marginalized groups have been treated in Germany in the past and how Germans are handling their integration today, both in terms of official policy and as reflected in the actions and attitudes of average German citizens. This is a story that includes tragedy and great human suffering, certainly; but it also includes a noteworthy record of progress toward tolerance and understanding. The goal at Michigan State is to convey a picture of Germany that is whole.

It is hoped that the following description of how issues of multiculturalism and diversity are integrated into course work at every level of the undergraduate program, from German 101 through the fourth year of the German major, may stimulate thinking about curricular reform in German at other institutions.[1]

First Year: Multiculturalism in Beginning German

Students who enroll in the first course of beginning German at MSU confront the issues of diversity and multiculturalism in German society already in the first days and weeks of the course. This exposure to a diverse German society alerts students at the outset of their study of German to the reality of contemporary German society and lays the foundation for instructors who teach German in the second-, third-, and fourth-year program. The majority of students in first-year German are fulfilling a language requirement, which at MSU is either one or two years, depending upon the student's major. Because most of the students in first-year German will not continue beyond the second year, we have a special responsibility to expose them to critical issues of German language and culture. At the same time, we see a more diverse group of students at the beginning level than we do at the third- and fourth-year level, and this guides the selection of materials and topics to be presented in the beginning course.

The primary focus regarding the treatment of issues surrounding diversity and multiculturalism at the first-year level is to present students with images and information reflecting the diversity of German culture. This begins with some reflection on stereotypes about American society. The centerpiece of our first-year curriculum is *Vorsprung* (Lovik, Guy, and Chavez 1997), which uses a wealth of visual materials to represent contemporary German society. All of the following examples are taken from *Vorsprung*.

The textbook introduces the treatment of diversity in German society by addressing the students' own notions about themselves. This assumes that students bring a variety of cultural stereotypes to the classroom with them, and the book works with these to dispel the myths and to develop an awareness of the differences. Very early on in the program, students are presented with several common stereotypes about Americans, as exhibited in Figure 1, in which eating habits, linguistic skills, and the tendency to smile often are viewed as problems.

In addition to this explicit means of presenting stereotypes, more subtle ways are also employed to suggest that both the learners of German as well as the speakers of German may be a more diverse group of people than students typically believe. Whereas most of the characters throughout the book are clearly mainstream, not all are. Afro-Germans and wheelchair-bound individuals, among others, are presented visually, as shown in the frames in Figure 2.

Similarly, conscious attempts have been made not to exclude any students from identifying with the language and the culture. Special effort has been made to provide students with the language they might need to describe themselves, e.g., "braune Augen" (brown eyes), "krauses Haar" (kinky hair), as shown in Figure 3.

Figure 1

Figure 2

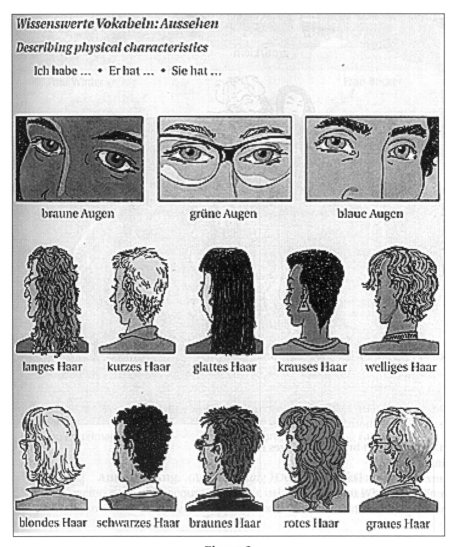

Figure 3

This attempt to provide inclusive vocabulary extends to language that many students need to describe their family situation, such as "Halbbruder" (half brother) and "Stiefmutter" (stepbrother), or sexual orientation, such as "schwul" (gay) and "lesbisch" (lesbian). The issue of multiculturalism in German society is directly addressed in Chapter 6 (of 12 chapters). The decision to position the topic of multiculturalism in the first half of the textbook was not arbitrary, but was done to ensure that those students who might not continue with German would at least have had the exposure to this topic. Addressing multiculturalism in German society necessarily shifts the focus away from the students in the class to German society, although not exclusively. This unit utilizes a text "Am Kopierer," written by a Turkish-German university student, Birsen Kahraman, but in a previewing activity, students are also provided the language they need to talk about themselves. As preparation for working with the authentic reading, students are asked to identify their own heritage in the following activity.

1. *Zu welcher Gruppe gehören Sie?* (To which group do you belong?)

    a. Ich bin europäischer Abstammung. (I am of European descent.)

    b. Ich bin asiatischer Abstammung. (I am of Asian descent.)

    c. Ich bin afrikanischer Abstammung. (I am of African descent.)

    d. Ich bin indischer Abstammung. (I am of Indian descent.)

    e. Ich bin hispanischer Abstammung. (I am of Hispanic descent.)

    f. Ich bin gemischter Abstammung. (I am of mixed descent.)

(*Vorsprung*, 233)

The text itself describes the experience of Turkish-Germans who are seen as non-German, based on their appearance, but who have been raised in Germany and consider themselves German. In a chance encounter with a German student at the photocopy machine, the speaker repeatedly shows her frustration at the German student's failure to recognize who she is. The following photo (Figure 4) clearly shows the dual images of Turkish-Germans. The mother in head scarf, who is holding a German Schulranzen (school bag), is juxtaposed with her daughter on her first day of school, who is holding her Schultüte (cone-shaped bag containing candy presented to children on their first day in school).

Figure 4

Following the reading, a brief cultural note on "Ausländer in Deutschland" (foreigners in Germany) attempts to highlight for students the critical role that foreigners have played in the German economic system as well as the animosity expressed by some to their presence in Germany. The information on foreigners concludes with a graph of 19 national groups found in the German workforce. The German reaction to marginalized groups in German society that is most familiar to Americans, and most difficult to deal with—the Holocaust—is treated in Chapter 7. This topic is juxtaposed with the rise of Neo-Nazi groups. Chapter 12 takes up the issue of diverse ethnic groups in Germany from the perspective of citizenship rights. Using a fictional Turkish worker, students are informed of the fundamental citizenship differences between the U.S. and Germany. Although many Turkish workers originally came to Germany seeking employment, as shown visually in Figure 5, their children do not automatically receive German citizenship, which has contributed to their second-class status in modern Germany.

This visual presentation of issues of diversity and multiculturalism in German society in the first-year German class at MSU is not intended to provide all the information or to answer all the difficult questions that students have. Hopefully, however, they will have been encouraged to continue their study of German beyond the first year, where they will have the opportunity to look at some of the same issues in more depth.

Figure 5

Second Year: Blacks in Germany? A Scene from
Die Ehe der Maria Braun

Sections of fourth-semester German at MSU have different thematic focuses. The course as a whole is designed to bridge the traditional gap between intensive language study at the intermediate level and the integrated courses dealing with language, culture, and literature in the curriculum that begin in the fifth semester.

One section of German 202 that is taught almost every semester is entitled "Abenteuer Bundesrepublik" (adventure Germany) and presents an overview of the development of Germany from 1945 to 1990 in the context of intensive review of the grammar, structure, and vocabulary of basic German. The four skills are practiced using textual material (literature, documents, video, and film) that deals with the cultural and historical development of post-World War II Germany. The course includes numerous segments dealing with issues of multiculturalism and diversity, such as the Holocaust, the Nuremberg trials, "De-Nazification," *"Gastarbeiter"* (guestworker), *Radikalenerlaß* (decree concerning radicals), Neo-Nazis, Mölln and Solingen, refugees and *Asylanten* (asylum seekers), literature written by "foreigners," the debate about dual citizenship for foreigners, and the role of women in the FRG.

For the first part of the course, covering the period from 1945 until 1954, the Film *Die Ehe der Maria Braun* (Rainer Werner Fassbinder, 1978) can effectively be used to introduce virtually all of the major problems facing Germany and Germans in the period immediately after the war: the hardships for civilians, the fate of the *Heimkehrer* (returnees), the economic "miracle" and the Adenauer era, the role of women in postwar Germany, and the rapid rise of materialism as it relates to the problem of *Vergangenheitsbewältigung* (coming to terms with the past). In Fassbinder's film, Maria Braun has a relationship with a black GI named Bill, whom she meets working as a hostess in a club for American soldiers. Bill is portrayed sympathetically as he falls in love with Maria. In a pivotal scene in the film, Maria's husband unexpectedly returns from a prisoner of war camp and finds Maria and Bill in bed. In the ensuing confrontation, Maria strikes Bill on the head with a bottle, killing him.

In one brief scene in the film, which lends itself well to classroom use, Maria and Bill walk up a hillside. Bill is teaching Maria English words, pointing to various objects, including facial features, for example "These are your lips." The scene culminates in a bittersweet exchange, when Bill says, "I am black; you are white," and Maria repeats verbatim, saying, in effect, that she is black and Bill is white. The intimacy between the racially mixed couple and the linguistic confusion in the scene serve as an effective springboard for initiating class discussion about the problems of foreigners in Germany, beginning with the question of Germany's traditional ethnic makeup, the presence of other ethnic groups in Europe, the awareness—or lack of it—among Germans of people of color, and how the degree of language competence relates to issues of power and marginalization.

The scene from *Maria Braun* is memorable and serves as a good reference point throughout the semester for changing perceptions among Germans about foreigners in the Federal Republic. Toward the end of the course, the short film *Der Schwarzfahrer* (Pepe Danquart, 1992) serves as an effective counterpoint to the scene in *Maria Braun*. The setting is Berlin in the early 1990s. Various scenes of the film reveal a metropolitan population that is diverse in every respect, including ethnically. The film's denouement, a confrontation in a streetcar between an embittered, racially intolerant older German woman and a young black, is both amusing and telling. Times have changed, it seems, and although none of the other passengers speaks up on behalf of racial tolerance, their sympathies are clearly with the young man who is Black and not with the woman, who is summarily removed from the streetcar for failing to produce her ticket. She is a *Schwarzfahrer,* but so, literally, is the young man, and he, not the woman, will continue his journey through Berlin—thus the film's implicit message.

In another segment of the course, portions of texts from the anthology *Farbe bekennen* (Oguntoye, 1992) are used to illustrate the presence of second- and third-generation "foreigners" in the Federal Republic. Particularly effective is the story of Helga Emde, "Als 'Besatzungskind' im Nachkriegs-deutschland" (occupation babies in postwar Germany), a story which might well have ensued from the liaison between Maria and Bill in *Die Ehe der Maria Braun*. The following passage, which again relates "otherness" to language competence, serves as a good basis for a final class discussion on the issue of racial tolerance in Germany, on the progress that has been made, and on the problems that remain.

> Ich habe auch eine dunkle Hautfarbe, bin aber Deutsche. Das glaubt mir niemand ohne weiteres. Früher sagte ich, um vor weiteren Fragen Ruhe zu haben, ich sei von der Elfenbeinküste. Ich kenne dieses Land nicht, aber es klang für mich so schön weit weg. Und nach dieser Antwort kamen auch keine Fragen mehr. So dumm sind die Deutschen. Ich konnte den Leuten jede Geschichte erzählen, Hauptsache, es klang ihnen fern und exotisch. Nur daß ich Deutsche bin, glaubte mir niemand. Wenn ich auf die Bemerkung "Ach, Sie sprechen aber gut deutsch" antworte: "Sie auch", bleibt den Leuten der Mund offen stehen.
>
> Erst in der letzten Zeit ist es mir gelungen, in meine eigene braune Haut zu schlüpfen und mich zu meinem Schwarzsein zu bekennen.... Ich kann meine weißen wie auch meine schwarzen Anteile akzeptieren und empfinde darin keinen Bruch. (111f.)

(I have a dark skin, too, but I am a German. No one believes that, without some further explanation. I used to say that I was from the Ivory Coast, in order to avoid further questions. I don't know that country, but to me it sounded so nice and far away. And after this answer, I didn't get any more questions either. Germans are that ignorant. I could tell people any story I wanted to, the main thing that it sounded foreign and exotic. But no one ever believes that I am German. When I respond to the remark, "Oh, you speak German so well" by saying "So do you," people's mouths drop open.

It's only recently that I have been able to feel more comfortable in my brown skin and come to terms with my blackness . . . I can accept the white part of me as well the black part and without feeling any breaks between them.)

Third Year: "Identity and Memory: Jewish Experience in Postwar Germany"

History in Contemporary Germany

When students of German arrive at the third-year level in the MSU program, they are certain to have received some information about ethnic minorities in German-speaking countries. The inclusion of multicultural elements in beginning and intermediate course materials is increasingly pronounced as both native German speakers and Americans struggle to understand and embrace the diversity of their own cultures, as the MSU model clearly demonstrates. In a third-year course on contemporary German culture, which carries as its sole prerequisite four semesters of language instruction, students have the opportunity to build on their basic awareness of cultural differentiation in Germany and to explore related issues through the lens of history. This approach reflects a conscious decision to depart from the common "smorgasbord" or "theme-of-the-week" model that one finds in many culture courses foregrounding current events. Such a model reinforces the temporal vacuum within which most American students live; that is, it constructs a world in which events of today are conceptually isolated from reflection upon the deeply embedded historical contexts out of which they arise.

In light of these concerns, German 340 foregrounds the role of history in the constitution of postwar German social, cultural, and political identities. Against the backdrop of a general twentieth-century German history text,[2] students analyze a wide array of materials revolving around critical, recurring issues that have defined both Germanys since World War II; these texts highlight difficult cultural problems of history, memory, and remembering, both in the public realm of politics and mass movements and in the shaping of individuals' life experiences. As they reflect upon the significance of the experiences of National Socialism and the Holocaust for Germans, students are encouraged to locate and identify continuities across the divide of 1945. Because the idea of the persistent presence of the past is a basic organizing principle of the course, rather than a laundry list of topics that must be covered, the course structure is flexible enough to incorporate a multitude of changing materials over time.

Jewish Voices: Complex Constructions of Individuality and Community

One of the pivotal texts used in the course is Peter Sichrovsky's (1987) *Wir wissen nicht was morgen wird, wir wissen wohl was gestern war*,[3] a collection of conversations with "young" Jews—i.e., children of Holocaust survivors and/or émigrés—living in West Germany and Austria. By focusing on Jewish voices in the present, students are encouraged to question the dominant model that divides Germans and Jews as separate and mutually exclusive groups; they are also forced to recognize that the discourse about Jews in Germany cannot be contained by the Holocaust itself. Students consistently identify this two- to three-week section of the course as one of their favorites, and its pedagogical advantages are indeed many, starting with form and language. The volume consists of interviews that have been edited into coherent first-person narratives (in the style of *Protokolliteratur*). This narrative form renders the text linguistically accessible without the need for glossing, and also enables students to establish points of identification with the various speakers quite readily.

Another pedagogically useful aspect of the text is its novelty; most students admit that they had never before entertained the possibility that there are still (or again) Jews *living* in Germany. By running counter to student expectations, Sichrovsky's book helps to undermine their received notion that Jews as "others" are absent from German society today. Finally, and equally powerful, are the differences that emerge among the Jewish German and Austrian speakers themselves: from the undying rage toward mainstream German society expressed by Fritz, a successful lawyer, to the positive identification that Tuvi has found as a German police officer; from the nearly scornful rejection of the Jewish community (and of all labels) by David, a teenager living in Berlin, to the solace found by a young Viennese woman, Helen, in the orthodox religious community. These widely differing relationships to Jewish cultural, ethnic, and/or religious heritage push students to grapple with the limitations of any monological interpretation of history and any monolithic construction of a group identity. As we work through this section of the course, the instructor can take advantage of the structure of Sichrovsky's accessible interviews and enact extended role-play exercises with students, assigning them the voices of the book in an almost endless variety of combinations. Gradually, they come to recognize the hard work involved in the negotiation of multiple, conflicting cultural identities.

Memory/Remembering

The people whose stories are contained in Sichrovsky's book have chosen to live in Germany/Austria in the shadow of the Holocaust. Rather than focus on the terror of the Nazi era, we discuss the impact that the past has had on a generation of living Jews for whom the Holocaust is a defining memory. These people struggle to grasp their position in German society by seeking access to their parents' (largely buried) memories, by embracing or rejecting aspects of Jewish and/or German culture. The context in which we read these stories is crucial: namely, in a fifteen-week course that presents a variety of other texts documenting non-Jewish Germans' struggles with identity and memory. By juxtaposing Sichrovsky's volume against other texts, the course consciously aims to complicate students' understanding of what it means to self-identify as German and to avoid the easy categorization of Germans and Jews into the roles of perpetrators or victims—indeed, as living or dead.

As they conclude this section of the course, students are given a writing assignment that builds on the dimension of memory—i.e., the personal process of integrating history into one's life—and takes advantage of the accessibility of the first-person narrative form. This essay requires them to recognize the constructedness of a life, by way of the process of remembering; here, students are allowed to incorporate their own life stories in the interpretive process ("Was bedeutet Erinnerung für Sie? Welche Funktion hat der Prozeß des Erinnerns—welche Funktion haben Erinnerungen selber—in Ihrem Leben?" ["What does the concept of memory mean to you? How are both the process of remembering, and memories themselves, important in your life?"]), while they are also forced to acknowledge the distance between their experiences and those of the Germans they have come to "know" in the course ("Was bedeutet Erinnerung für die Menschen, deren Geschichten wir bisher gehört bzw. gelesen haben? Welche Rolle spielt Erinnerung in ihrem Leben?" ["What does the concept of memory mean to the people whose stories we have read this semester? What role does remembering play in their lives?"]).

With the combination of materials and activities described above, German 340 links political and personal history with identity-building in the specific context of postwar Germany. It is the goal of this course to provide students with a way to begin thinking about cultural difference that is not contained by straightforward self/other dichotomies (e.g., visible ethnic markers, linguistic difference),[4] and to give them both the factual background and conceptual framework for further exploration of specific multicultural phenomena, both in foreign cultures and in their own.

Third-Year Business German: German for Business and Economics: Incorporating Issues of Diversity

A central focus of the business German program at MSU has been, since its inception in 1978, the integration of cross-cultural awareness into the curriculum, including issues of diversity. The rationale for the incorporation of such issues into the two-semester, third-year level sequence entitled "Advanced German: Business Emphasis" is threefold:

1. it reflects primary values of MSU's German program;
2. it is an important component of a liberal arts education which is generally not covered in courses in the business, engineering, and other professional school curricula from which students are drawn; and
3. such cross-cultural awareness is in increasing demand from American employers as they become more deeply involved in globally interdependent markets.

The latter point is supported by a 1994 Rand Corporation publication, *Developing the Global Workforce,* which deals with the impact of the global economy on the human resource needs of American companies. It addresses the need for cross-cultural competence in future employees who must be able to both understand the profound changes from national to international economic activity, as well as respond to specific international opportunities. Employees must now not only understand the internationalized business environment, but also how to apply functional knowledge in that environment. The development of cultural and ethnic tolerance is absolutely essential for all members of the American workforce if the United States is to remain competitive in today's global markets.

Cultural and ethnic tolerance is integrated throughout the textbook used for the MSU business German sequence, *German for Business and Economics* by Paulsell and Gramberg (1994). The works of cultural anthropologist Edward T. Hall provide the theoretical foundation for the exercises and activities (1959, 1966, 1981). In Volume I: *Die Volks- und Weltwirtschaft,* activities focus on the development of cultural awareness in general and on areas of economic activity as manifestations of certain deeper layers of culture. In Volume II: *Die Betriebswirtschaft,* there is further development of cross-cultural awareness skills and an application of those skills to organizational structure, marketing, and management practices.

An example of the integration of cultural awareness comes from Chapter 11 of Volume I, entitled "Herausforderung für Europa." In the *Kulturverständnis* section of this chapter, students are introduced to Hall's schema for interpreting target culture behavior in the context of the target culture, C2, not in the context of their native culture, C1. They learn that the ease of understanding another culture is inversely proportional to the importance that culture places on "silent language" and "hidden dimensions," i.e., nonverbal aspects of communication. They are familiarized with Hall's "Cultural Continuum," which places the U.S. and Germany on the "low context" end of the spectrum and China and Japan, for instance, on the "high" end.

The students are then introduced to an exercise which incorporates a chart drawn from a *Spiegel* survey "Profil der Deutschen" (Augstein, 1991). The survey shows that certain foreigners are more "sympathischer" than others, with rankings provided, in order, for French, Americans, Austrians, Gypsies, Russians, Jews, Poles, and Turks. Not surprisingly, the French, Americans, and Austrians were the only groups who received relatively high ratings; the Turks the only group with a negative rating.

Students are then asked to respond to some questions, using the *Spiegel* graph, along with a recent graph from the Globus Kartendienst, showing the expansion of the EU as projected in 1997—with Poland, the Czech Republic, Hungary, Slovenia, Cypress, and Estonia requesting entry into the EU. Here they must apply Hall's schema of "Sympathie/ Feindlichkeit" to the projected expansion.

The building of cultural and ethnic tolerance does not, of course, begin or stop with this one example. This is a continuation of the presentation of these issues which runs through the entire two-volume textbook. Thus, this is but one small example of the numerous activities and exercises in "German for Business and Economics" which focus on developing cross-cultural awareness, including ethnic and cultural tolerance, while encouraging students to apply the new skills to the world of business and economics.

Fourth Year: Dedicated Course to Marginalized Groups in German Society

GRM 440 Perspectives of Cultural Difference is an advanced undergraduate/ beginning graduate level course dedicated to the study of marginalized groups in German society through history. It is paired with GRM 441 Perspectives of Mainstream Culture in a thematic grouping where the instructor chooses required texts (written, oral, or visual) based on their social origin or content. These two courses are found among a group of four selectives (the others being an introduction to the study of literature and a linguistics course contrasting German and English structures), two of which are required for the German major. Any of these courses, however, are open to any student with appropriate language proficiency to handle texts, discussions, and examinations in sophisticated German. As such, the advanced German curriculum at MSU does not organize its text-based courses according to genre, author, or period, as is the case at most institutions.

GRM 440 can be viewed as a course in German studies or cultural studies that focuses on texts produced by marginalized in groups in society. It stresses the fact that German culture is not monolithic. Similar to almost any culture, it is composed of many parts, each sharing to a greater or lesser degree in the values, beliefs, and fantasies of the broader culture, and each harboring special concerns, values, beliefs, traditions, and history that provide a special commonalty that differentiates it from that broader culture. In addition, the course includes marginalized groups from several historical epochs:

1. Turkish women in present-day Germany,

2. peasants in the Middle Ages,

3. Afro-Germans throughout history,

4. Jews in Annheim 1900-1941,

5. gays and lesbians 1869-1933, and

6. German immigrants to the U.S. in the nineteenth century.

(Texts used and a detailed syllabus can be found on the World Wide Web at <http://www.msu.edu/~mcconegh/ grm440/>.) Although many have an easier time relating to marginalized groups in contemporary German society, groups from earlier periods are included in the hope that the distance in time, place, and familiarity will allow students to better apprehend the mechanics of marginalization and how those mechanics are useful tools in studying marginalization regardless of when it did or will occur.

The texts chosen to introduce students to marginalized groups in society, focus on the dynamic relationship between marginalized groups and the mainstream, the locus of social power. The special value of GRM 440, however, does not lie in a focus on the status of minorities as victims through German history. Instead, the course employs a framework through which the students discover agency and voice among the marginalized, e.g., how could and did the groups actively respond to the limitations imposed upon them by the mainstream and adopt strategies by which they could survive? And further, how did the historical moment and the personal values of individuals within the group influence which "survival strategies" were adopted? The chapter "Notes on the Management of Difference," pages 73-101 of Carmen de Monteflores's (1986) *Contemporary Perspectives on Psychotherapy with Lesbians and Gay Men,* is especially useful in constructing the framework for discussion of every text studied in class.

The framework begins with an outline of the strategies that serve the interest of the mainstream by differentiating and marginalizing groups within the broader society. These include:

1. The imposition of a marginalizing group identity: What characteristics identify a group? What should one expect of a member of that group? (stereotyping);

2. The exclusion of members of the marginalized group by
   a. characterizing them as morally inferior, physically ugly
   b. characterizing these traits as inborn and irreversible
   c. criminalizing behavior whose goal is the integration of the marginalized group into the mainstream;
3. Limited integration: permitting members of the marginalized group to integrate with the mainstream, but only as long as it serves the interests of the mainstream
   a. for entertainment purposes (sports, curiosity pieces, song, dance)
   b. for economic benefit (cheap labor force)
   c. for the benefit of one's soul, moral colonization (do-gooder syndrome).

The class reads and interprets texts against this initial frame. What evidence can one find in the expressions of marginalized groups of these mainstream strategies? How is the group being characterized, being exploited, being disenfranchised?

The second frame used gets beyond the status of minorities as passive victims and investigates the ways that they deal with their marginalization. We analyze texts from the point of view of the marginalized, identify the strategies chosen by group members, list the conditions and values that led to the particular choices, and explore the consequences of the decision. Students look for some combination of the following six strategies often used by minorities to interact with individuals from the more powerful mainstream cultural group:

1. Acquiescence: acceptance of the identity imposed by the mainstream, playing the role, "good daughter" syndrome (e.g., Turkish women follow patriarchal family rules and restrictions);
2. Assimilation or "passing:" external differences with the mainstream are minimal; change of the individual to become like the mainstream; rejection of marginalized identity (Jews who become Aryans in the Third Reich);
3. Belief in special status: characteristics that marginalize are reinterpreted as assets (e.g., Nazis truly value black-skinned people because they need them to appear in propaganda films);
4. Self-ghettoization: requires self-sufficient community, strong group bonds—usually religious (e.g., Amana community in Iowa);
5. Confrontation: marginalization is no longer tolerable; external situation must be changed (e.g., peasants in 1525; homosexual groups around 1900);

6. Flight: marginalization no longer tolerable; individuals must remove themselves from their surroundings, either by leaving the country, a flight into fantasy (books, insanity), suicide (e.g., Jews in the Third Reich).

Students usually do not find all these methods equally attractive or acceptable. In general, today's students favor assimilation as a strategy; some prefer confrontation. Few, however, find acquiescence or flight to be viable alternatives, even when they come to understand the personal values that might lead to those choices or the dire consequences for individuals who choose other options. Impatience with an author's or character's choice of strategy, however, prompts self-reflection about one's own values, the privileges and limitations one experiences in one's own life, and the degree to which one is a risk-taker. (The strategies of both mainstream and marginalized groups are presented in greater detail on the web at <http://www.msu.edu/~mcconegh/grm440/strategien.htm>.)

In sum, a semester-long course on multicultural aspects of German society can lead to exceptional educational experiences at an advanced level in the German curriculum. Students repeatedly note how GRM 440 ties in with courses in other fields and how the course relates directly to questions they are facing in their own lives. It is necessary, however, that students coming through a German program have encountered the issues and vocabulary of multiculturalism at earlier stages in their course of study so that they know what to expect out of an advanced-level course of this type and so that they are linguistically prepared to profit from the readings and discussions. It is heartening to take part in a program where such a learning process takes place from the very beginning and to work with a group of colleagues who share common goals and objectives in making German a more realistic and relevant course of study for our undergraduates.

Notes

1. Each of the authors of this article is responsible for one of the courses described: Beginning German (Lovik), Fourth Semester German (Peters), Third-Year Contemporary German Culture (Mittman), Third-Year Business German (Paulsell), Fourth-Year Course on Marginalized Groups in German Society (McConeghy).
2. Mary Fulbrook, *The Divided Nation: A History of Germany 1918–1990* (1992). While students read this book in English, a series of German worksheets assists them in processing the most pertinent ideas, builds vocabulary in the target language, and facilitates the transition from reading at home in English, to discussing in class in German.
3. Sichrovsky has also edited another volume of interviews with children of Nazis, entitled *Schuldig geboren* (1987). The decision to use *Wir wissen nicht was morgen wird* is based on its greater potential to break up monolithic stereotypes of Germans as a homogeneous ethnic group; the latter, while extremely interesting and worthwhile in its own right, arguably runs the risk, at this level of instruction, of merely reinforcing students' equation of Germans and Nazis.

4. This is not to say that some of the voices in Sichrovsky's (1987) book do not have their own run-ins with cultural stereotyping of this sort; one such example is Susan, the daughter of American immigrants who has returned to Germany and is taken for a Turk because of her dark hair and distinct facial features.

References

Augstein, Rudolf, ed. 1991. *Das Profil der Deutschen: Was sie vereint, was sie trennt.* Hamburg: Spiegel Verlag.

Fulbrook, Mary. 1992. *The Divided Nation: A History of Germany 1918–1990.* New York: Oxford UP.

Die Unterrichtspraxis–Teaching German. (1994) Developing the global workforce. Rand Corporation.

Hall, Edward T. 1959. *The Silent Language.* Garden City, N.Y.: Doubleday.

——. 1966. *The Hidden Dimension.* Garden City, N.Y.: Doubleday.

——. 1981. *Beyond Culture.* New York: Anchor Books.

Lovik, Thomas, Guy, Douglas, and Chavez, Monika. 1997. *Vorsprung: An Introduction to the German Language andd Culture for Communication.* Boston: Houghton Mifflin.

Montefiore, Carmen de. 1986. *Contemporary Perspectives on Psychotherapy with Lesbians and Gay Men.* New York: Plenum.

Oguntoye, Katharina, Opitz, May, and Schultz, Dagmar, eds. 1986. *Farbe bekennen: Afro-deutsche Frauen auf den Spuren ihrer Geschichte.* Berlin: Orlanda Frauenverlag.

Paulsell, Patricia R., and Gramberg, Anna Katrin. 1994. *German for Business and Economics, Volume I: Die Volks- und Weltwirtschaft* and *Volume 2: Die Betriebswirtschaft.* East Lansing: Michigan State UP.

Schulz, Renate A. 1993. "Profile of the Profession: Results of the 1992 AATG Membership Survey." *Unterrichtspraxis–Teaching German* 26.2: 226-252.

Sichrovsky, Peter, ed. 1987. *Schuldig geboren.* Köln: Kiepenheuer & Witsch.

——, ed. 1985. *Wir wissen nicht was morgen wird, wir wissen wohl was gestern war: Junge Juden in Deutschland und Österreich.* Köln: Kiepenheuer & Witsch.

10
Creating a Professional Development Network for Prospective and Inservice Foreign Language Educators
Unifying Diverse Expertise

Deborah Wilburn Robinson
The Ohio State University

Introduction

Beginning in the 1980s, dissatisfaction with American schooling led to a series of reform initiatives across the nation. One such effort, the Holmes Group, critically examined all aspects of our educational system from teacher education programs to professional development for veteran teachers, administrators, and university faculty. In the end, Holmes advocated partnerships between universities and K-12 schools called Professional Development Schools (PDS). PDS educators investigate teaching and learning processes with an eye towards improving every facet of schooling for students and teachers.

While such partnerships have been in existence for some time at The Ohio State University in other content areas, the Foreign and Second Language Professional Development Network (FSLPDN) is in its inaugural year. This paper will report on the formation of our PDN based on a review of the literature, stories from the field, and the results of a study conducted with area teachers.

Review of the Literature

In the mid-1980s the Holmes Group, a consortium of deans at a variety of Colleges of Education, began the dialogue on reforming the American education system. Their first report, *Tomorrow's Teachers* (1986), laid out the competencies that teachers need in order to teach the next generations of children successfully. *Tomorrow's Schools* (1990) delineated how K-12 education might be reconceived in collaborative partnerships with Colleges of Education. The boldest move by these deans was to examine their very own teacher preparation programs with a critical eye. What emerged was a candid report, *Tomorrow's Colleges of Education* (1995), in which it was admitted that these programs needed help in preparing future teachers. Stakeholders from the university and the schools, it was proposed, would work together in a collaborative relationship that far exceeds the university methodologist/university supervisor/cooperating teacher triad model that has driven teacher preparation to date. Rather, theory and practice would be more fully integrated throughout a future teacher's tenure in a teacher education program. Practicing teachers and teacher educators would exchange roles often, with the teacher serving as the methods instructor and the professor working with students in the teacher's classroom. Administrators and curriculum specialists would also facilitate the preservice teacher's metamorphosis into a prepared novice teacher. In short, the whole educational community would nurture prospective educators while concurrently focusing on improving teaching and learning through inquiry and open dialogue. These two endeavors would lead teachers and teacher educators to center on their own continuous professional development as well.

The recommendations from these three reports formed the basis for the goals that drive what have come to be known as Professional Development Schools:

- High quality professional preparation
- Simultaneous renewal
- Equity, diversity, and cultural competence
- Scholarly inquiry and programs of research
- Faculty development
- Policy initiation

Once the basic goals for Professional Development Schools were set, a variety of PDS endeavors appeared in the U.S. The case studies and personal narratives that emerged from these initiatives provide useful guidance for others who wish to implement the goals of PDS.

Lessons from the Field: Studying PDS Initiatives

Goodlad and Sirotnik (1988) delineate issues and problems that potentially plague school-university collaboration. Contextual factors, such as differences in prestige and status, as well as differences in demands, expectations, and reward systems in the school and in the university can lead to an atmosphere of distrust and to eventual misunderstandings when members of these two cultures interact. Differences in organization of annual and daily work schedules at the two levels, issues of authority and responsibility, and the need for governing and managing structures that represent all interests in the partnership are also factors that need to be taken into account when planning for successful collaboration. The authors caution, however, that "productive tension" (p. 207) between the two cultures is necessary for true reform. Without such tension, the result is often merely doing the old, better.

Goodlad and Sirotnik (1988) also examine the tension between giving voice to participants and reaching some sort of closure. Similarly, tension exists between the nagging feeling that change is threatening and the willingness to engage in the process of change so as not to waste precious time and energy. In concluding, Goodlad and Sirotnik propose the "need for an agenda specific enough to bind participants in a common enterprise but general enough to allow for individuality and creativity" (p. 219).

Rosaen and Hoekwater (1990) trace the inception of their PDS at Michigan State University and explain how educators in a nearby elementary school, university faculty, and graduate teaching and research assistants came to realize their PDS through genuine collaboration. Clarifying terms, roles, philosophies, and purposes continued over a six-month period while the work of the collaborative ensued. Once again the lessons seem clear: The projects in which partnerships engage are not tasks in isolation. Participants must build trust and understand each other's cultures.

Garfinkel and Sosa (1996) describe an early attempt in their foreign language teacher education program to incorporate the premises of the Holmes Model. As with other authors, these educators highlight the prerequisite of a trusting, mutually beneficial relationship before universities and schools can reach a point of true collaboration. Furthermore, the authors contend that human rather than material resources ensure the success of such partnerships. It follows that the most precious of these human resources is one's time.

The 1996 summer issue of *Contemporary Education* contains 19 articles documenting the experiences of PDSs affiliated with Indiana State University and its 15 PDS sites. The table of contents reveals several of the themes articulated above. The first section of the issue underscores the need to clarify the purpose of PDSs. Section two chronicles how PDSs are seeking deeper, institutionalized change in schools and university classrooms. In the third section, select PDSs reflect on how they have achieved true collaboration, and they assess anecdotally the processes and products of PDS involvement. The final section calls for a more systematized evaluation of PDSs and gives examples from both the quantitative and qualitative traditions of what such evaluation might entail.

In a volume to be released this spring (1998), Johnston Brosnan, Cramer, and Dove chronicle the conception and implementation of veteran and start-up PDSs across a variety of content areas at The Ohio State University. The text addresses three areas of concern. The first section describes the political and theoretical context from which PDSs emerged. Next, the challenges of working collaboratively to effect change are discussed. The third section assesses the consequences or outcomes of PDSs based on research and development. The research and experience represented in this work have inspired to a great extent the conceptualization of our own Foreign and Second Language Professional Development Network (FSLPDN) in central Ohio.

Developing OSU's PDN: A Research-Based Approach

In the state of Ohio, as in many others, prospective foreign language teachers receive initial certification to teach in K-12 classrooms. English as a Second Language (ESL) validation must be added to an existing certificate in a foreign language, math, social studies, or any other content area. Ohio State's teacher education program, now at the M.Ed. level, involves practicum experiences in a variety of levels (elementary, middle school, and high school) in a variety of program formats (foreign language experience or FLEX, foreign language in the elementary school or FLES, immersion, and traditional secondary programs), across a variety of languages (10), in diverse settings. Given the nature of OSU's preservice education program, it was recognized that an extensive network of foreign language educators would be needed to represent all levels, languages, types of programs, and contexts. In the spring of 1997, therefore, a research study was conducted to seek answers to the following questions:

- Who are the potential participants in our PDN?
- Which areas of expertise do potential participants bring to the PDN?
- Whose responsibility is it to meet the goals set forth by the Holmes Group?
- What kinds of resources are available in the field to meet these goals?
- What kinds of resources would the university need to provide to meet these goals?
- How do we unify the diverse expertise of university faculty, graduate teaching assistants and researchers, K-12 teachers, and administrators into a meaningful PDN based on the Holmes Partnership goals?

Examining the Possibilities: A Teacher Survey

In teaching, we are instructed to start where the learners are. In order to assess more adequately where K-12 teachers' opinions fall in relation to the goals of PDS partnerships, then, a survey was sent to 350 foreign and second language teachers in select Franklin County schools (see Appendix A). A parallel survey form was also sent to each building administrator. Administrators were instructed either to respond to the survey themselves or to pass it to a curriculum specialist or supervisor. The county schools, which include both Columbus Public and Diocesan schools, were selected for the project because they have traditionally served OSU's preservice teachers for their field experiences and student teaching practica. In exchange for mentoring OSU's future teachers, inservice practitioners receive fee waivers to attend university classes (usually three credit hours per quarter). ESL, immersion, and foreign language teachers were included in the research, for as Tedick and Walker (1996) have consistently stressed, much can be accomplished when the fields work together. Surveys containing information from OSU's office of student teaching were mailed to each department chair or lead teacher in the schools. These contacts were asked to distribute the surveys to each second or foreign language educator. Ninety of the 350 surveys were returned.

Whereas 66 surveys were sent to administrators, only nine were returned. Ironically, when a call for support letters for the Professional Development Network was issued to these same administrators, 26 responded. Because of the low rate of return for the administrator survey, results will not be discussed in this report.

Results of the Teacher Survey

The first part of the survey sought demographic information about the respondents. The first question concerned languages taught by each teacher. Note that total responses often exceed 90 because some teachers teach more than one language. Although Italian, Japanese, and Chinese are also taught in the schools, no teachers from these languages responded to the survey.

Spanish	French	German	Latin	ESL	Russian	ASL	Arabic	Swahili
52	34	8	5	3	2	2	1	1

Next, respondents indicated their current teaching levels. Again it is evident that some teachers work across levels:

No Response	K-6	Grades 6-8	Grades 9-12
1	2	26	70

The low number of K-6 respondents is disappointing but mirrors the fact that area schools do not offer many early language learning opportunities.

There are two total immersion schools and a handful of FLES programs in the community. Still, the data are troubling in that participation by ESL instructors was lower than expected. Given the historical separation of our respective fields, however, this finding is not overly surprising.

The results of the third question demonstrate that the trends reported in the literature concerning the graying of the teaching force (Schrier 1993) are occurring in our content area as predicted:

No Response	0-5 Years	6-10 Years	11-15 Years	16-20 Years	21+ Years
2	9	19	14	20	26

As these figures indicate, the majority of the teachers who responded to the survey will likely retire from teaching within the next five to ten years. One of the main reasons for inaugurating a PDS is to tap into these veteran teachers' wealth of experience before they retire.

The next four items on the survey were designed to determine the degree to which area teachers are invested in the concept of continuous professional development. It is encouraging to see that so many teachers engage in life-long learning and professional development experiences that extend beyond requirements for initial certification and renewal. The first item on the highest level of education to date yielded the following information:

BS/BA	M.Ed.	MA	MA + 30	Ph.D.	No Answer
34	3	29	21	2	1

Twenty of the 90 respondents were enrolled in a degree program at the time of the survey and 42 were enrolled in continuing education courses. For those who were not enrolled in such courses, 30 said that they intended to take additional courses in the future. One hundred percent of the sample, then, was either enrolled in university courses or planned to take additional classes in the future. On the one hand, this is encouraging given the goals of self-renewal and professional development delineated in the Holmes Partnership literature. On the other hand, it would be naïve to believe that all of these educators are motivated by the intrinsic rewards of further learning. One must also consider the impending changes in state licensure and the increased compensation tied to continued education. These data are nevertheless important in that it is easier to form partnerships when participants already interact with each other, regardless of the motivation.

The issue of power has consistently emerged in the PDS literature as an important factor. Consequently, it was also necessary to determine if potential participants in our collaborative held positions of power and further, to ascertain the nature of these positions. Only 25 of the 90 respondents reported holding any such position. Of these 25 respondents, 19 were department chairs, 4 were mentor teachers, one was a textbook chair, and one a teacher leader.

Time is another of the major concerns of establishing and maintaining a PDS. In an effort to determine the teaching loads of potential PDN participants, respondents were asked to report the number of classes they teach each day out of the possible number of class periods. Twenty of the survey participants indicated that their institution is on a block-schedule format. Consequently, the reader should interpret the results with caution, bearing in mind that teaching two blocks would be equivalent to teaching four traditional classes. Nonetheless, the range of teaching responsibilities and the variety of scheduling practices across the county is remarkable: Teachers in the county teach from two to seven classes (or blocks) per day and they spend from 16%-100% of their time in direct instruction. The majority of teachers teach five or six classes a day. Only three of the respondents have no time in their schedules for other activities besides teaching. Fifteen of the participants have only one period during the day for other activities. The vast majority, however (71 of 90), have two or more periods a day in which they do not teach. The survey, however, did not ask about lunch duty or study hall assignments.

It is crucial to ascertain the teaching and duty loads of PDN participants for several reasons. First, if preservice teacher development is to be a collaborative venture, field teachers must have time to offer feedback and guidance. Similarly, if methods classes are to be co-taught on site, with real K-12 students, it is helpful to have a pre-observation conference with the teacher as well as a post-observation phase. During these times, the teacher can explain his/her thinking, orient university students to what they might see during the lesson, and state the objectives for the lesson. Following the class observation, it is more valuable to review the lesson with the teacher shortly after a classroom visit than to wait several days to talk about it in a seminar at the university.

The second reason these data are so critical is that inservice teacher development is a time-consuming proposition. The reader may recall that the Holmes Partnership goals call for simultaneous renewal of university faculty and teachers in the schools, built upon a program of inquiry into teaching and learning as they work with preservice teachers. Attending workshops or designing inquiry projects must be fashioned to account for teaching responsibilities.

The final two questions from the demographic portion of the survey sought to establish how many potential PDN participants had already hosted university preservice teachers. Sixty-five of the 90 reported having worked with observers and/or methods students:

No Answer	1-3 Students	4-6 Students	7-10 Students	11+ Students	Many
3	45	9	1	2	5

Of the 90 respondents, 55 have also served as cooperating teachers for student teachers. The breakdown follows:

One	Two	Three	Four	Many
27	14	11	2	1

The fact that 25 teachers had never hosted university students and that 35 had never been cooperating teachers supports the notion that a network for professional development and the improvement of teaching and learning through inquiry is an idea whose time has come. Both teachers who already had ties to the teacher education program as well as teachers with no such previous relationships took the time to respond to the lengthy instrument.

The first part of the survey, then, yielded vital baseline information for establishing our PDN. We learned that there is a wealth of experience in the field and that the participants are committed to their own professional development. Because so few teachers who responded to the survey are in positions of power, strong ties will have to be made with administration in order to assure the institutionalization of the network. Finally, the heavy teaching loads of most teachers leave little time for other activities during the school day. Nonetheless, 71 of the 90 have two or more periods in the day that could be partially devoted to working with the network.

Participants' Beliefs about Teacher Development Responsibilities

Having come to understand who the potential network members might be, it was also important to ascertain their beliefs about responsibilities, roles, resources, and areas of research for our PDN. The second section of the survey, therefore, asked participants to respond to prompts regarding these areas. The first of these prompts consisted of 16 descriptors or objectives from the preservice component of the teacher education program. Survey participants were asked to indicate whether they believe that the responsibility falls to the university teacher education program (TEP), to the cooperating teacher, or to a joint partnership between the two. Respondents could weight their answers by circling US for "more the job of the university" or SU for "more the job of the school." The prompts and the number of respondents are given in Appendix B, Section I.

An analysis of the responses reveals that in all but two cases, participants believe that university and inservice K-12 personnel should share preservice teacher education responsibilities equally. Respondents tended to favor more school involvement with curriculum development and assessment geared toward the National Standards and state model curriculum. In addition, the incorporation of realia, authentic materials, and technology into instruction was deemed more the task of the schools. Moreover, teachers considered it more their responsibility to work with prospective teachers on strategies for discipline and classroom management and on communication with parents and fellow educators. Not surprisingly, when items were of a more theoretical nature, for example, making content accessible to students through an understanding of developmental factors, second language acquisition processes, and/or the importance of background knowledge in comprehension, respondents tended to favor more responsibility on the part of the university. Similarly, K-12 educators favored more university involvement where inquiry and reflection into the teaching/learning process was the focus. Finally, teachers also considered the articulation of a teaching philosophy and the need for lifelong learning more the purview of the university. Taken together, these data give powerful justification for the Holmes Partnership model of preparing prospective teachers.

Roles and Resources in Teacher Development

If the responsibility for preparing future teachers is to be shared, the roles of the various partnership participants must be ascertained. The next series of questions on the survey investigated just how respondents view the possible roles open to them in conceiving a network around Holmes Partnership goals. A summary of the responses is given in Appendix B, Section II. Overall, the results indicate that teachers are most willing to carry out roles and engage in activities with which they are most familiar. Practicing teachers are willing and eager to assume more active roles in both their own professional development and, more importantly, in working with preservice teachers. For example, 83 of the 90 teachers indicated that they would be willing to observe and provide feedback to preservice teachers and to serve as cooperating teachers. In addition, they reported a fairly high degree of interest in playing a role in student teaching seminar discussions. Teachers also were interested in participating in professional development activities such as inservice seminars or special courses designed for foreign language teachers. From their responses, it is evident that the National Standards in Foreign Language Education Project (1996) as well as Foreign Languages: Ohio's Model Competency Based Program (1996) have attracted the attention of the state's foreign language educators. Teachers want information on new techniques for proficiency-based teaching and assessment. They understand that foreign language learning is truly a lifelong enterprise and they want opportunities to increase their own proficiency in all of the skill areas. Furthermore, they know that technological savvy is crucial to maintaining pace with and accessing knowledge and they are aware of the power of the new media to provide links to authentic materials throughout the world. Finally, the idea that *all* learners should be in our foreign language classes has begun to take root, and teachers want to learn new instructional strategies to accommodate "nontraditional" learners.

Beyond the major trends in the responses to this section of the survey, there were a number of single responses for various professional development topics and these can be organized into two main categories. Under the first category, which focused on research in the field and grant writing, topics suggested by participants included constructivism, student-centered curriculum, motivation, applied linguistics, and reducing fossilization. The second category of responses consisted of issues critical to teacher survival such as discipline and management strategies and ways to increase communication with parents, school board members, and colleagues.

Though they wished to be included in preservice development, teachers understandably expressed somewhat less interest in taking on roles and activities that do not conventionally fall into their range of experiences. For example, 42 of the 90 teachers reported that they would be willing to teach sample lessons in university methods courses and 57 indicated an interest in participating in action research with colleagues or preservice teachers. Though less robust than the responses to more familiar roles, the figures are quite encouraging and demonstrate that a good number of teachers are willing to take on risks and assume new roles and responsibilities in the PDN. In fact, one native speaker teacher suggested a new role not mentioned on the survey by offering to work with novice teachers as a language role model.

The field educator role, that of a teacher who continues teaching in his/her classroom with additional administrative and teaching responsibilities in the network, was the least appealing to this sample of respondents. Only 18 teachers indicated that they would be willing to serve in this capacity. (See Appendix C for a more detailed description of the position.) Given the busy schedules of many of the survey participants and the fact that the role is conceptually new to many foreign and second language educators, a response of 18 should also be viewed optimistically.

In summary, the data indicate clearly that practicing teachers are willing to continue in more traditional roles such as observing student teachers, serving as host teachers, and participating in inservice activities. The added dimensions of providing formal feedback to student teachers and helping to organize inservice education opportunities further demonstrate that the goals of Holmes Partnerships PDSs are tenable and timely.

The next question on the survey was designed to determine whether respondents had understood the reconceptualization of preservice teacher development. Asked whether they would be willing to work with a prospective teacher over the course of an academic year, 68 of the teachers agreed, 12 said that they would not be willing to work with a preservice teacher for an entire year, 3 were unsure, and 7 failed to respond.

For those who did not wish to work with students for such an extended period, reasons varied. Concern over a yearlong commitment, the stressful nature of working with student teachers, the need to rebuild their own programs, and impending retirement were some of the reasons teachers gave.

One respondent felt that university students should work with a variety of teachers during their tenure in a teacher education program. (In fact, students will work with a minimum of three.)

Some teachers who indicated that they were open to the idea of working with prospective teachers nevertheless had some reservations. Concerns focused on the need for training as mentors, lack of access to e-mail to facilitate communication, and other commitments that would preclude full participation. Similarly, the following comment captures the essence of another potential problem: "One year can be a long time if two people disagree on critical issues."

For other teachers who responded positively, however, there were no reservations:

"It allows the cooperating teacher and potential student teacher to build a relationship prior to actual student teaching."

"Why didn't someone think of this before?"

"This allows for cohesion for the teacher education program and more continuity for our students [in K-12 schools]."

To address some of the potential problems associated with the student teacher-cooperating teacher dyad, respondents were also consulted on whether inservice and preservice teachers should be screened prior to participation in the network. Overwhelmingly, 80 of the 90 respondents support a review process for cooperating teachers (5, no; 5, NA). Suggestions for screening included interviews, résumés, surveys, class observations, attitude measures, self-evaluation, and compatibility screenings. Participants also delineated criteria for consideration of a teacher as a cooperating teacher.

By far, the most recommended criteria for cooperating teachers are the desire to work and a history of working with preservice teachers. Respondents recognize that although one might be a master teacher him/herself, it takes a unique individual to be able to deconstruct the teaching act, look at practice objectively, and allow novices to grow into good teachers through practice and feedback. Survey participants also described the personal characteristics that a good cooperating teacher might exhibit. While some of these traits represent inherent qualities (e.g., stability, flexibility, enthusiasm, and openness), others could be learned and practiced (e.g., professionalism, organization, communication skills). In addition, respondents felt that a strong command of methods, theory, and technology in relation to standards set in our field was critical for any cooperating teacher. It follows that veteran teachers with an established record of competent teaching and demonstrated high language skills would exhibit these criteria. Survey participants also suggested that these teachers be recommended, either by administrators or by their teaching peers. Other criteria focused on classroom management and rapport with students. A record of continued professional development and service to the profession coupled with belief in the philosophy of the network were also desired characteristics for serving as cooperating teachers. Finally, understanding university expectations for preservice teacher development was cited as a necessary element to being a successful model teacher.

In response to a parallel query about whether student teachers should be screened prior to the student teaching practicum, 74 of the 90 considered it a good idea, 11 did not consider it a good idea, and 5 gave no response. Suggestions for screening included presenting sample lessons, interviews on teaching and learning, self-evaluation, surveys, portfolios, and "retraining" for those who do not pass the screening. Some respondents also offered criteria for potential screening: Personal qualities (being a "people person," integrity, sincerity, maturity, stability, professionalism, enthusiasm, organization, dedication, cooperation, initiative, responsibility, work ethic, commitment) were most often listed as important for predicting success (38 responses). These attributes mirror those in the literature (Howey and Zimpher 1996). Personal readiness to assume teaching duties (9 responses) and the recommendations of veteran educators (7 responses) were other criteria mentioned by teachers. Similar to their recommendations for cooperating teachers, survey respondents also felt that compatibility with host teachers and school sites was fairly important (7 responses). Skill in lesson planning (5 responses), current methods (4 responses), and discipline techniques (4 responses) were also cited. The relatively low response rate by teachers with regard to these latter skills is encouraging, as it is precisely these skills that future teachers wish to perfect in university classes and field placements. Finally, an adequate GPA (4 responses), caring about children (4 responses), and communication skills (2 responses) were reported as desirable criteria.

In the next question of the survey, K-12 teachers were asked what they felt they could do to facilitate the development of preservice teachers. Whereas 23 participants chose not to respond, those who did provided a clearer picture of additional roles for teachers in a PDN. The most mentioned function was that of sharing. Inservice teachers cited willingness to share both concrete ideas, lessons, and materials (33 responses) and more abstract expertise such as their understanding of schools, knowledge of the learning process, skills in time management, and organizational strategies (33 responses). Next, respondents suggested that they could facilitate preservice teachers' development both by being observed and by observing with feedback (29 responses). In a related vein, participants indicated that they could mentor prospective teachers through exposing them to a supportive atmosphere and through providing them with access to children (28 responses). Three teachers also stated that they could help by learning from their preservice teachers. Finally, veteran educators spoke of offering specific programs (American Sign Language) or inservice seminars (accepting other languages/cultures, interviewing practice) to help novices.

While the survey participants felt they could facilitate preservice teachers' growth in a number of ways, they also listed areas where they wished additional help or resources for working with a preservice teacher. Forty-five respondents provided insights into this dimension of a potential PDN.

According to the most frequently offered suggestions, the area most in need of clarification is the university's expectations in all dimensions of fieldwork. Teachers want to meet to discuss goals and requirements. They want to receive written instruments and lists related to tasks that must be completed and they want to understand more fully how to supervise this process. Finally, they want to watch demonstration lessons and see what the university deems appropriate in terms of lesson planning in order to match their personal views with those of the university. Furthermore, 12 respondents wish to maintain close contact with university personnel and some also wish to be involved in methods classes and seminars to ensure that fieldwork and coursework converge. Beyond these two crucial areas, teachers want help with innovative methods (7 responses), integrating technology into classes (6 responses), and strategies for teaching others about classroom discipline (3 responses). Meeting prospective teachers prior to placement and having potential teachers tour schools were also suggested (2 responses) as ways to help veteran teachers help novices. Lastly, teachers wish for what all busy professionals need—more time.

When asked in which areas they wished additional help or resources to further their own professional development, survey respondents listed diverse issues. Whereas 37 respondents offered no suggestions, the remaining teachers consistently mentioned five areas. First, 16 teachers wished additional help with technology. They want to learn how to use it and how to convince administrators that technology is essential not only in math and science classes, but also in foreign language settings. Second, 15 participants wanted to learn about new methods, theories, activities, and materials for communicative language teaching. In the third category, 11 educators cited learning about these areas through inservice meetings and workshops. In relation to their own language proficiency, 11 respondents also spoke of the need for study abroad opportunities for teachers. It is clear that teachers are getting the message that their own language proficiency is inextricably linked to realizing the goals of the communicative language classroom. While educators seek formal study in their efforts to make their classrooms more proficiency based, they also wish to learn from each other. The fourth resource, then, was released time to observe each other and to share authentic materials (11 responses). The fifth most-cited area (8 responses) was help in matching assessment to instruction, particularly through the use of portfolios. Teachers understand that if the communicative classroom is to be institutionalized, assessment must be congruent with teaching.

After these areas, teachers also want opportunities to receive graduate credit for participation in the network and through innovative and flexibly scheduled courses for teachers (3 responses). In addition to these most frequently identified areas, a number of other specific areas for further support were listed. Although many of these could be addressed through discussions of methods, theories, and activities, others must be addressed through tailored workshops and inservice sessions. For example, appeals were made to help teachers establish American Sign Language programs, create professional development opportunities germane to immersion education, and focus inservice on the middle school years. The complete listing of suggestions for this item of the survey can be found in Appendix B, Section III.

Inquiry into Teaching and Learning

The third major area of concern for Professional Development Schools is a research agenda to inform teaching and learning. Inquiry provides the focus for both preservice and inservice teacher development. While observing a prospective teacher, veterans also reflect on their own practice. As young teachers observe their mentors, they too are actively involved in seeing theory in practice and arriving at grounded conclusions about teaching and learning. In order to determine the issues teachers would be willing to explore, survey participants were asked to prioritize areas of action research that the PDN might investigate. Before prioritizing the list, respondents were invited to add their own suggestions. Participants were then instructed to choose five issues and to prioritize them 1-5 with 1 being the highest. (Some respondents wrote only 1s, 2s, or 3s.) The themes that appeared as the top five choices for each respondent, along with the frequency with which they were chosen, are reported in Appendix B, Section IV.

Not surprisingly, the themes for possible areas of inquiry parallel those for professional development. The central theme focuses on finding ways, through classwork and homework, for increasing linguistic and cultural proficiency of students. Moreover, teachers wish to explore ways to incorporate technology into instruction. Another popular avenue of exploration was researching various grouping and scheduling strategies and their effects on proficiency. Still other suggestions focused on incorporating theories and practices more consonant with current thinking in the areas of curriculum and assessment where research is still lacking. With more and more programs serving inclusion students, teachers also wanted to engage in inquiry centered on how to serve these students better. With regard to their own professional development, teachers also thought that a productive subject for research would be documenting the effects of peer supervision on teaching. Other original suggestions offered by teachers are included at the end of Appendix B, Section IV.

Are K-12 Teachers Ready for a Professional Development Network?

Two final questions of the survey sought to discover whether K-12 teachers were committed to the idea of a network. The first queried whether teachers support the idea of university teacher educators, graduate teaching assistants and researchers, preservice teachers, classroom teachers, administrators, and curriculum specialists working together for everyone's ongoing professional development. Overwhelmingly 87 of the 90 respondents said yes; only one participant responded in the negative, and two participants offered no opinion.

The second question asked for justification and clarification of the previous question. The participant who answered no expressed the following opinion on professional development: "Professional development should be a 'personal quest' so I have concerns for the inclusion of so many parties in professional development." The follow-up question for participants who answered "yes" asked which obstacles would have to be overcome or what conditions would need to exist for the network to become a reality. By far, the most-cited obstacles were time constraints (42 responses) and money for released time (19 responses). Conditions that would ensure the success of the network included issues of respect for all K-postsecondary educators (37 responses) and convenience of actual meeting times (22 responses). Further conditions mirror those cited in the literature: The network must be well organized with a clear agenda and means of assessment (8 responses). Other factors that survey participants found important to the success of the network were incentives for network personnel (4 responses) and the relative status of foreign languages in schools (3 responses). Appendix B, Section V lists the complete summary of responses to this question.

Unifying Diverse Expertise

The results of this survey, combined with themes from the literature, inform how our PDN has been conceptualized to date. What follows is a chronicle of establishing the network—including the goals we have set and a description of how the roles of the participants were established.

Accompanying the survey was a notice for a June 1997 meeting to discuss survey results and brainstorm about the network. During this initial meeting, which attracted 32 area educators in K-16 foreign and second language programs, participants listened to colleagues from both the university and from area schools who had experience in PDSs. A former principal, now the coordinator of PDSs for the university, presented the goals of Holmes Partnerships and explained how pleased he was that the voices from the field were finally being heard. He also addressed the difficulties involved in institutionalizing a PDS but challenged the group to do so. Second, the Associate Dean of Programs from OSU's College of Education, who has worked closely with PDS initiatives, informed the group about the State Department of Education's new licensure standards. She explained how our PDN might tie into these requirements for both preservice and veteran teachers. Next, a social studies field educator shared his experiences as a practicing teacher involved in a PDS, highlighting how his work in the collaborative has given him a renewed interest in all aspects of teaching. He lauded the model for having forced him to engage in inquiry. Having chapters published in the literature on PDSs has given his students renewed respect for him and his own view of himself as an educator has grown. In closing, he also warned of the time commitment involved but said the effort was well worth the sacrifice.

After these testimonies, I reviewed what the literature had to offer on PDSs. We did not skirt the hard issues of mutual respect, true collaboration, the various systems of reward, or the perceptions of prestige. The themes of collaboration, professional development, and inquiry from the Holmes literature were also fully explained, though no recipes were given for how these themes might play out in our new venture. Next, I explained the successes of another school-university partnership that had been formed specifically to address issues of high school-to-college articulation and assessment in French, Spanish, and German programs in the state. Several of the educators who had participated in the project were present and corroborated the benefits of project participation. (See References for the Collaborative Articulation and Assessment Project [CAAP] (Birckbichler, Robison, Wilburn Robinson 1995) for more information.) We proposed to build upon CAAP and expand the network by bringing in ESL, Latin, Less Commonly Taught Language, and K-8 teachers.

After these presentations and discussions, the participants formed three, smaller working groups to deliberate what they considered possible for the partnership in view of the survey results, testimony from other PDS participants, the literature on PDS, and the impending state initiatives for pre- and inservice teachers. One group focused on preservice teacher development. To frame the discussion, the group was given the following questions:

- In what kinds of activities should student teachers engage?
- What kind(s) of feedback do they need?
- What role(s) can teachers in the field play in developing prospective teachers?
- What roles should field educators have?

The second working group focused on inservice teacher development and worked with the following guiding questions:

- What kinds of workshops/courses would you like to see offered?
- Who should organize them?
- Should it always be the university's responsibility?

The third group's task was to discuss how the inquiry component of the PDN might function. Again, questions were provided to start the discussion:

- What kinds of projects might we wish to engage in?
- What kind(s) of help do inservice teachers need to engage in inquiry?

After lunch, each group gave a report and then opened up discussion for further suggestions from the other groups. Subsequently, we set our goals over the next three years to focus on preservice teacher development, inservice teacher development, and inquiry, respectively. To this end, teachers were invited to sign up to review the university's methods syllabi and suggest topics and readings. Furthermore, those willing to allow methods students to visit their classrooms and observe them, for example, employing techniques for cooperative learning, teaching grammar in context, or working with literature, were also asked to sign up.

In August 1997, four graduate teaching assistants and I reviewed the applications we had received for the six field educator positions. Using a rating scale, we made our decisions based on years of experience, evidence of continued professional development, letters of support from other teachers and administrators, and service to the profession. These six inservice teachers, reflecting the languages, levels, and teaching contexts needed to provide a good variety of experiences for preservice teachers, were also given copies of methods syllabi and asked for input for revision.

When our first group of M.Ed. students began in mid-September, the syllabi were revised to reflect the input of practicing teachers. Methods-class visits to local classrooms were embedded in the syllabi. Field educators had each chosen a week during which they would co-facilitate the seminar with our GTA assigned to the course.

Methods students have been in their host teachers' classrooms since the second week of the quarter to complete a series of focused observation tasks. Most recently, classroom teachers hosting our methods students (some of whom are also our field educators) and I have been revising the list of mini-teaching experiences to be accomplished in the field near the end of the methods course sequence. Similarly, field educators have been helping to redefine the final assessment for the M.Ed. Rather than a four-hour paper-and-pencil exam, students will compile a portfolio over their last two quarters in the program and participate in an oral defense of the contents.

In order to monitor and advise the work of the partnership, we have formed a steering committee with representatives from both the university and the public schools. Steering committee members consider and rule on all matters of policy in such areas as accepting new participants into the network, revising programs, preparing field educators, ensuring that the goals of the Holmes Partnership Model are in the forefront of our thinking, evaluating programs, and initiating grants. Moreover, the group decided that, based on the survey data, we would also work on choosing host teachers; screening student teachers; communicating clear expectations on roles, duties, and responsibilities; and establishing better means of communication.

If this sounds like an ambitious agenda, it is. We will need at least a full year to realize the basic functions of the network. But the rewards have been encouraging. One of the host teachers, in conjunction with her technology educator, is fashioning a Web project for the M.Ed. students. A field educator, in his own right a successful grant writer, is working with me to secure funding for PDN endeavors. The Spanish Department, responding to the need for courses to increase language proficiency, offered a late afternoon course on pronoun usage. One faculty member alone could not possibly manage these disparate elements of collaborative pre-and inservice professional development, especially where responsibilities extend beyond the M.Ed. to other area program levels.

Conclusion

The Foreign and Second Language Professional Development Network for pre- and inservice educators at The Ohio State University and in Franklin County schools is in its inaugural year. We continue to meet to give the Holmes Partnership Model a distinct flavor based on the needs in our content area. The data from the survey discussed herein allow more than intuitions to inform our PDN. We know the wealth of human potential we have to work with as well as the limitations. We are convinced, however, that by combining the expertise that each of us possesses, we will succeed in making a difference in the professional development of us all.

Acknowledgments

The Central States Grants and Fiscal Development Committee and the Associate Dean of Programs, College of Education, The Ohio State University, supported this study. Many thanks are also due Hilary Raymond for her technical assistance in the preparation of this article, and to Teresa Benedetti, Anna Gelinas, and Hilary (all graduate students in the Foreign and Second Language Education Program) for their input on the surveys. I would like to thank the reviewers for their constructive comments on this manuscript.

References

Birckbichler, Diane, Robison, Robert, and Wilburn Robinson, Deborah. 1995. "A Collaborative Approach to Articulation and Assessment," pp. 107-123, in Gail Crouse, ed., *Broadening the Frontiers of Foreign Language Education*. Report of the Central States Conference on the Teaching of Foreign Languages. Lincolnwood, IL: National Textbook Co.

Contemporary Education. Summer, 1996. Vol. 67, No. 4.

Corl, Kathryn, Harlow, Linda, Macián, Jan, and Saunders, Donna. 1996. "Collaborative Partnerships for Articulation: Asking the Right Questions." *Foreign Language Annals* 29, 2: 111-124.

Freeman, Donald. 1996. "Renaming Experience/Reconstructing Practice: Developing New Understandings of Teaching," pp. 221-241, in Donald Freeman and Jack Richards, eds., *Teacher Learning in Language Teaching*. NY: Cambridge University Press.

Foreign Languages: Ohio's Model Competency-Based Program. 1996. The Ohio Department of Education, Columbus, OH.

Garfinkel, Alan, and Sosa, Carol. 1996. "Foreign Language Teacher Education in a Professional Development School," pp. 97-121, in Zena Moore, ed., *Foreign Language Teacher Education: Multiple Perspectives*. Lanham, MD: University Press of America, Inc.

Goodlad, John, and Sirotnik, Kenneth. 1988. "The Future of School-University Partnerships," pp. 205-225, in Kenneth Sirotnik and John Goodlad, eds. *School-University Partnerships in Action: Concepts, Cases, and Concerns*. NY: Teacher's College Press.

Holmes Group. 1986. *Tomorrow's Teachers*. East Lansing, MI: Holmes Group.

————. 1990. *Tomorrow's Schools*. East Lansing, MI: Holmes Group.

————. 1995. *Tomorrow's Schools of Education*. East Lansing, MI: Holmes Group.

Howey, Kenneth, and Zimpher, Nancy. 1996. "Patterns in Prospective Teachers: Guides for Designing Preservice Programs," pp. 465-505, in Frank Murray, ed., *The Teacher Educators Handbook: Building a Knowledge Base for the Preparation of Teachers*. San Francisco: Jossey-Bass.

Johnston, Marilyn, Brosnan, Patricia, Cramer, Don, and Dove, Tim, eds. 1998. *Ohio State University Professional Development Schools: Context, Challenges and Consequences*. New York: Teachers College Press.

National Standards in Foreign Language Education Project. 1996. *Standards for Foreign Language Learning: Preparing for the 21st Century*. Yonkers: NY: American Council on the Teaching of Foreign Languages.

Rosaen, Cheryl, and Hoekwater, Elaine. 1990. "Collaboration: Empowering Educators to Take Charge," pp. 144-151, *Contemporary Education,* vol. 61, No 3.

Schrier, Leslie. 1993. "Prospects for the Professionalization of Foreign Language Teaching," pp. 105-123, in Gail Guntermann, ed., *Developing Language Teachers for a Changing World*. Lincolnwood, IL: National Textbook Co.

Tedick, Diane, and Walker, Constance. 1996. "R(T)eaching All Students: Necessary Changes in Teacher Education," in Barbara Wing, ed., *Foreign Languages for All: Challenges and Choices. Northeast Conference Report*. Lincolnwood, IL: National Textbook Co.

Appendix A
Teacher Survey

Dear Foreign Language Teacher:

The following survey is funded by the OSU College of Education and the Central States Grants and Fiscal Development Committee. As OSU moves to the M.Ed. level for initial licensure, we must formalize relationships we have had with all of you in the past. Results from the survey will help inform the creation of a professional development network for preservice and inservice teachers, administrators, and university personnel. The purposes of creating such a network are to provide a forum for ongoing professional development on issues specific to foreign language teaching and learning and classroom-based inquiry through collaboration.

Language(s) Taught:

Levels/grades:

_____ immersion _____ K-6 _____ 6-8 _____ 9-12

Number of years of teaching experience:

_____ 0-5 _____ 6-10 _____ 11-15 _____ 16-20 _____ 21+

Highest level of education to date:

_____ BA/BS _____ M.Ed. _____ MA _____ MA + 30 _____ Ph.D.

Are you currently enrolled in a degree program? _____ yes _____ no

Are you currently taking continuing education courses? _____ yes _____ no

If no, do you plan on taking continuing education courses in the future?

_____ yes _____ no

Do you hold an administrative position within your school? (Chair, resource teacher, mentor, supervisor) _____ yes _____ no

If yes, please explain. _____

Number of classes you currently teach each day _____ out of _____ possible periods.

Is your institution on a block schedule? _____ yes _____ no

If yes, please explain. _____

Have you hosted an observer/methods students during the last five years?
_____ yes   _____ no

If yes, how many? _____ 1-3   _____ 4-6   _____ 7-10   _____ 11+

Have you been a cooperating teacher for a student teacher during the last five years?   _____ yes   _____ no

If yes, for how many student teachers?   ___ 1   ___ 2   ___ 3   ___ 4

For the following list of descriptors, indicate whether you believe the responsibility falls to the university teacher education program (TEP), to the cooperating teacher, or to a joint partnership between the two. If you would like to weight your answers, circle US for "more the job of the university" or SU for "more the job of the school."

U = university TEP   E = equal responsibility
US = university plus school   SU = school plus university
                                 S = school

1. Developing curricula based on the National Standards and State Model.
   U   US   E   SU   S

2. Developing lesson and unit plans as well as accompanying materials.
   U   US   E   SU   S

3. Understanding how to translate content knowledge into student-centered lessons.
   U   US   E   SU   S

4. Integrating technology into foreign language classrooms.
   U   US   E   SU   S

5. Incorporating authentic materials and realia.
   U   US   E   SU   S

6. Developing tests/assessments (conventional and alternative forms of assessment).
   U   US   E   SU   S

7. Developing discipline strategies and classroom management.
   U   US   E   SU   S

8. Reaching all learners (learning styles, inclusion, being attentive to diverse populations).
   U   US   E   SU   S

9. Learning how to communicate with parents, colleagues, school boards.

     U   US   E   SU   S

10. Understanding developmental stages of learners (emotional, social, and cognitive).

     U   US   E   SU   S

11. Understanding second language acquisition (e.g., error correction, proficiency levels, communicative language teaching).

     U   US   E   SU   S

12. Understanding theoretical issues in designing listening, speaking, reading, writing, and culture lessons (e.g., importance of background knowledge, matching the task to proficiency level).

     U   US   E   SU   S

13. Developing a philosophy of teaching/learning.

     U   US   E   SU   S

14. Reflecting on practice through journaling, conferencing, peer discussions.

     U   US   E   SU   S

15. Learning how to conduct classroom-based inquiry.

     U   US   E   SU   S

16. Understanding the need to participate in lifelong professional development (study/travel abroad, conferences, workshops, coursework).

     U   US   E   SU   S

As we conceive our professional development network, what would you be willing to do?

- Teach specific lessons showcasing your expertise in university methods. classes. _____ yes _____ no

- Observe and provide formal feedback to preservice teachers.

  _____ yes _____ no

- Serve as a cooperating teacher. _____ yes _____ no

- Participate in student teaching seminar discussions.

  _____ yes _____ no

- Participate in action research projects with colleagues and/or preservice teachers on issues of importance to you and to the field at large.
  _____ yes   _____ no

- Organize and/or attend inservice seminars based on professional development needs of FL educators.   _____ yes   _____ no

- Take courses specifically designed for FL teachers.
  _____ yes   _____ no
  If yes, what topics would you like to see addressed?

  _____

  _____

  _____

- Serve as a field educator (see job posting in your district office).
  _____ yes   _____ no

- Other(s): _____

  _____

  _____

  _____

Would you be willing to work with a preservice teacher over an academic year? (Host for observation/methods during the fall, stay in contact via e-mail or in occasional seminars in winter, act as cooperating teacher during student teaching in spring.)   _____ yes   _____ no

Please explain your answer. _____

_____

Should cooperating teachers be screened?   _____ yes   _____ no

If so, based on what criteria? _____

_____

Should student teachers be screened?   _____ yes   _____ no

If so, based on what criteria? _____

_____

What do you feel you could do to facilitate the development of a preservice teacher?

_____

_____

In what areas would you like additional help/resources to facilitate working with a preservice teacher?

_____

_____

In what areas would you like additional help/resources to facilitate your own professional development?

_____

_____

Please rank, in order of importance to you, the following areas of action research that we as a PDN might choose to investigate. Please add your own suggestions to the list before you rank order. (1 = most important.)

_____ Types of pair and group activities (i.e., cooperative learning) that promote proficiency.

_____ Strategies for encouraging the use of the foreign language both inside and outside the classroom.

_____ Kinds of authentic listening and reading texts that promote proficiency.

_____ Kinds of homework assignments that are conducive to promoting achievement/proficiency.

_____ Utility, benefits, and/or practicality of incorporating technology into lessons.

_____ The effects of incorporating multiple intelligence or learning style theories in the development of FL curricula.

_____ The impact of alternative assessment practices on student communication and/or performance.

_____ Types of physical class configurations that best promote speaking.

_____ Kinds of authentic materials that are beneficial to promoting cultural awareness.

_____ The effect of process writing (prewriting, multiple-drafts, peer editing) on my students' writing proficiency.

_____ The effects of block scheduling on student achievement/placement scores.

_____ Methods that best benefit inclusion students in the FL classroom.

_____ The benefits of participating in peer (nonevaluative) supervision for FL teachers.

_____ Other(s)

Do you support the idea of university teacher educators, graduate teaching assistants and researchers, preservice teachers, classroom teachers, administrators, and curriculum specialists working together for everyone's ongoing professional development? _____ yes   _____ no

If no, why not? _____

_____

_____

_____

_____

_____

If yes, what obstacles would have to be overcome or what conditions would need to exist for this to become a reality? _____

_____

_____

_____

_____

_____

_____

Appendix B

Summary of Results to Selected Survey Items

This appendix provides a summary of responses to selected sections of the survey presented in Appendix A. Numbers that appear adjacent to response options refer to the number of respondents who selected that option or who mentioned a given item.

I. Where Responsibilities Lie in Preservice Teacher Education

For the following list of descriptors, indicate whether you believe the responsibility falls to the university teacher education program (TEP), to the cooperating teacher, or to a joint partnership between the two. If you would like to weight your answers, circle US for "more the job of the university" or SU for "more the job of the school.."

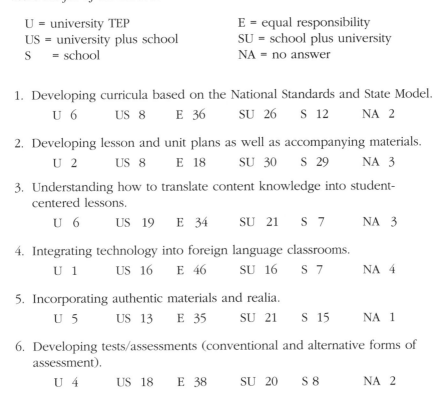

U = university TEP   E = equal responsibility
US = university plus school   SU = school plus university
S   = school   NA = no answer

1. Developing curricula based on the National Standards and State Model.

    U 6   US 8   E 36   SU 26   S 12   NA 2

2. Developing lesson and unit plans as well as accompanying materials.

    U 2   US 8   E 18   SU 30   S 29   NA 3

3. Understanding how to translate content knowledge into student-centered lessons.

    U 6   US 19   E 34   SU 21   S 7   NA 3

4. Integrating technology into foreign language classrooms.

    U 1   US 16   E 46   SU 16   S 7   NA 4

5. Incorporating authentic materials and realia.

    U 5   US 13   E 35   SU 21   S 15   NA 1

6. Developing tests/assessments (conventional and alternative forms of assessment).

    U 4   US 18   E 38   SU 20   S 8   NA 2

7. Developing discipline strategies and classroom management.

   U 2   US 8   E 33   SU 28   S 17   NA 2

8. Reaching all learners (learning styles, inclusion, being attentive to diverse populations).

   U 5   US 15   E 44   SU 16   S 5   NA 5

9. Learning how to communicate with parents, colleagues, school boards.

   U 2   US 9   E 34   SU 30   S 12   NA 3

10. Understanding developmental stages of learners (emotional, social, and cognitive).

    U 17   US 25   E 39   SU 6   S 0   NA 3

11. Understanding second language acquisition (e.g., error correction, proficiency levels, communicative language teaching).

    U 20   US 31   E 34   SU 3   S 0   NA 2

12. Understanding theoretical issues in designing listening, speaking, reading, writing, and culture lessons (e.g., importance of background knowledge, matching the task to proficiency level).

    U 21   US 42   E 19   SU 5   S 0   NA 3

13. Developing a philosophy of teaching/learning.

    U 12   US 26   E 40   SU 7   S 2   NA 3

14. Reflecting on practice through journaling, conferencing, peer discussions.

    U 19   US 23   E 35   SU 17   S 2   NA 4

15. Learning how to conduct classroom-based inquiry.

    U 10   US 29   E 30   SU 13   S 1   NA 7

16. Understanding the need to participate in lifelong professional development (study/travel abroad, conferences, workshops, coursework).

    U 6   US 15   E 56   SU 8   S 2   NA 3

II. Roles and Resources in Teacher Development

As we conceive our professional development network, what would you be willing to do?

Teach specific lessons showcasing your expertise in university methods classes.

        42 yes   42 no   6 no answer (NA)

Observe and provide formal feedback to preservice teachers.

        80 yes   8 no   2 NA

Serve as a cooperating teacher.

        83 yes   7 no

Participate in student teaching seminar discussions.

        72 yes   15 no   3 NA

Participate in action research projects with colleagues and/or preservice teachers on issues of importance to you and to the field at large.

        57 yes   22 no   11 NA

Organize and/or attend inservice seminars based on professional development needs of foreign language educators.

        76 yes   11 no   3 NA

Take courses specifically designed for FL teachers. (Suggested topics from respondents are collapsed into five categories.)

        71 yes   13 no   6 NA

New methods/materials to promote proficiency-oriented instruction.

Technology

Courses to improve teacher knowledge/proficiency of the target language and culture

Testing and assessment, including portfolios and rubrics

Teaching at-risk/special education learners, accommodating different learning styles

Serve as a field educator (see Appendix C for job posting)

        18 yes   38 no   34 NA

III. Professional Development Needs/Resources of Practicing Teachers

16 Using/acquiring technology

15 New methods/theory and application/materials/activities for the communicative classroom

11 Inservice/workshops/study-abroad language courses for teachers, especially in summer

11 Released time to observe others in field/share with others (e.g., bank of authentic materials)

 8 Development of assessments/portfolios

 3 University credit for participation in network, flexible scheduling of graduate courses, cost reduction for graduate courses

 3 More discipline/management strategies

 2 Culture inclusion/cultural celebrations in the classroom

 2 More help for immersion teachers' professional development

 2 Accommodating learning-disabled students, diverse populations in foreign language class

 1 Finding qualified substitute teachers

 1 Work in interdisciplinary curricular offerings

 1 Working with block scheduling

 1 Understanding state standards and curriculum development

 1 More informal dialogue with university

 1 Cooperative learning techniques

 1 Motivating students

 1 Developing learning centers

 1 Developing a program for teachers of ASL

 1 Help in offering ASL programs

 1 List of community resources

 1 More middle school program-specific professional development

 1 Convincing administration of need for new textbook

 1 How to justify foreign language study to students

 1 Supporting German language programs

IV. Possible Areas of Inquiry

54 Types of pair and group activities (i.e., cooperative learning) that promote proficiency

42 Strategies for encouraging the use of the foreign language both inside and outside the classroom

39 Kinds of authentic listening and reading texts that promote proficiency

37 Kinds of homework assignments that are conducive to promoting achievement/proficiency

35 Utility, benefits, and/or practicality of incorporating technology into lessons

31 The effects of incorporating theories of multiple intelligence or learning style in the development of foreign language curricula

29 The impact of alternative assessment practices on student communication and/or performance

28 Types of physical class configurations that best promote speaking

27 Kinds of authentic materials that are beneficial to promoting cultural awareness

26 The effect of process writing (prewriting, multiple-drafts, peer editing) on students' writing proficiency

16 The effects of block scheduling on student achievement/placement scores

13 Methods that best benefit inclusion students in the foreign language classroom

5 The benefits of participating in peer (nonevaluative) supervision for foreign language teachers

1 Strategies to encourage "equal time" of instruction for both boys and girls

1 Classroom management strategies

1 Motivating the foreign language learner

1 Effects of functionally organized programs on student achievement/placement scores

1 The impact of grading (A, B, C, 4.0, 3.5, etc.) on the foreign language learner and on language acquisition in the formal classroom setting

1 The progression of how students perceive and produce language (i.e., first lexical, syntax)

Appendix C
Call for Field Educators

What is a Field Educator?

A school-based teacher educator who continues teaching in his/her own class-room while also assuming responsibility for certain aspects of teacher development, including observation and feedback of preservice teachers, instruction in initial teacher preparation methods courses, entry-year support, and action research. Service in this role would be directly tied to professional development responsibilities in the College of Education at The Ohio State University, as well as enhance school-based professional development. This person works closely with faculty, graduate teaching assistants and graduate research assistants from the university, as well as other field educators and administrators in K-12 settings. The field educator serves for a period of no less than two years and no more than four years.

Responsibilities

Joint development and implementation of preservice, entry-year, and continuing professional development programs for prospective, beginning, and career teachers.

Provide inservice workshops

Help select cooperating teachers

Co-instructional and independent instructional responsibilities for courses offered in preservice, entry-year, and continuing professional development programs, including didactic, clinical, and field experiences.

Teach in methods courses

Lead seminars

Observation and feedback responsibilities as classroom supervisors for prospective teachers (in field experiences and student teaching).

Contributions to on-site collaborative inquiry in terms of action research and other appropriate research strategies including design and conduct of inquiry and appropriate dissemination and utilization of findings.

Collaborate with GRAs to organize and coordinate action research projects.

Provide inservice on incorporating results from research into classroom practice.

Continuing self-renewal in terms of staying abreast of current issues in language teaching and instruction.

Attend and present at conferences

Take courses

Candidate Qualifications

A field educator is a classroom teacher who:

- Desires to work on the professional development agenda of all foreign language pre- and inservice teachers.
- Has a strong commitment to his or her own professional development and is willing to engage in continued preparation for the role of field educator.
- Enjoys helping peers grow professionally and has engaged in joint problem solving and shared decision making with colleagues for the improvement of instruction.
- Holds or is working towards a master's degree in foreign language education, curriculum and instruction, or a related field. Has taught a minimum of five (5) years as a full-time foreign language teacher in K-12 settings and holds a valid teaching certificate.

Conditions for Appointment

Field educators will remain under contract with their current school districts, including salary and benefits. The university will provide stipends to field educators to compensate for approximately 70 hours per quarter of services rendered in the PDN as specified above. Field educators also receive fee waivers to attend university classes at a rate of 3-5 credits per quarter. Appointments follow the school district calendar for the academic year and are renewable contingent upon the success of the field educator and the PDN.

11
Spanish Dialect Variation
Language Diversity within the Spanish-Speaking World

Kathleen Wheatley
University of Milwaukee—Milwaukee

As foreign language teachers, we are in the unique position of being able to expose our students to diversity and to help them react positively to this diversity. In the foreign language classroom, students become aware that not everyone speaks their language, nor eats the foods that they eat, nor has the same type of daily schedule. However, as they learn about how the language and culture of another country differ from their own, the differences within the target language and culture are often overlooked, and students are given the impression that the target language and culture are much more homogeneous than they really are. If we hope to celebrate diversity in the language classroom, students should become aware of the diversity that exists within the target language and culture as well. In addition to increasing their understanding of the target language and culture, this awareness may also help them to become more accepting of diversity in their own language and culture.

In most language textbooks, little attention is given to language diversity within the target language. Instead, only the standard form of the language is presented, even though this dialect is spoken by only a segment of the population and does not represent the speech of many native speakers. The reasons for this are multiple. In the case of Spanish, which is spoken in so many different countries, it is most practical to teach a standard dialect which will be most easily understood by all speakers of the language, regardless of the region. In addition, the standard form tends to be spoken by more educated speakers, and it is the form used most often in the media. In addition, much of the language diversity that exists in the Spanish-speaking world is considered to be substandard by more educated speakers, and it therefore carries a certain stigma with it. Textbooks, consequently, present the most prestigious form to our students and ignore most of the variation that exists among dialects. This standard form may shift over time depending on social and political factors, but the focus on one correct way of speaking remains a constant. Such has been the case for Spanish over the last decades, where a shift has occurred from Castilian Spanish of Spain to American Spanish of the highland regions of Mexico, Colombia, and Peru as the standard dialect which is presented in most textbooks.

I do not question the wisdom of teaching the standard variety of Spanish to our students, but if we are truly committed to celebrating diversity, then the study of dialects within a language should be a component of our curriculum as well. If our goal is to have students be more tolerant and accepting of diversity, then we need to expose students to language differences and get beyond the stigmas that some of this variation has attached to it. In this paper, I will present examples of language variation in Spanish to which advanced students should be exposed in their language career. On a phonological level, I will examine the tendency towards loss or confusion of syllable and word-final consonants in some dialects. As a morphological example, I will discuss the variation that exists in the use of second-person pronouns. In the realm of syntax, I will describe the choice of third-person direct and indirect object pronouns. In all of these examples, I will demonstrate how the synchronic variation away from the standard is not in any way a corruption of the language. Instead, all of this variation can be explained diachronically, as tendencies within the historical development of the language from Latin to Spanish. In other words, languages are always changing, and this change results in a range of dialects which follow certain tendencies to a greater or lesser degree. In many cases, the most innovative changes carry the greatest stigma, but in some cases, the innovation becomes the standard form. As I will demonstrate below, the acceptance of any given innovation has more to do with the social and political status of the dialect in which the change occurs than with the validity of the change itself.

Elision of Word-Final Consonants

When comparing the phonological development of word-final consonants from Latin to each of the Romance languages, one finds a clear tendency towards the open syllable, CV, ending in a vowel rather than a consonant (Vincent 1988b: 37). This development has, for the most part, eliminated the final consonant in languages such as Portuguese (Parkinson 1988: 141), French (Harris 1988: 213), and Italian (Vincent 1988a: 283).

Spanish, however, has proven to be somewhat more conservative, maintaining a small group of word-final consonants: /-s, -n, -l, -d, -r/ in the standard form. However, the tendency towards an open syllable has continued in some Spanish dialects. Caribbean Spanish has gone the farthest in the effacement of final consonants, but other dialects, such as Andalusian and American coastal varieties, also share many of these characteristics (Lipski 1994). Some examples of this development include the aspiration or complete elision of syllable and word-final /-s/, as in libros, pronounced as [líbroh] or [líbro]; the confusion and/or elimination of syllable and word-final /-r/ and /-l/, as when parte is pronounced as [pálte] or [páte]; the velarization or loss of word-final /-n/, as in pan, pronounced as [pang] or [pa] with a nasalized vowel; and the weakening of both intervocalic and word-final /-d/, as when hablado is pronounced [abláo] and libertad is pronounced [libertá]. I will look at each of these tendencies in more detail below.

The syllable and word-final /-s/ is preserved in Castilian Spanish and in the highland regions of Mexico, Colombia, Ecuador, Peru, and Bolivia. The aspiration or loss of syllable and word-final /-s/ is widespread in Andalusia and in all of the coastal regions of Latin America (Canfield 1962), but its frequency is often determined by sociolinguistic factors (Barrutia and Schwegler 1992: 214-225), such as the age and level of education of the speaker, as well as the type of situation the speaker is in (formal/informal). The aspirated form still preserves a remnant of the original /-s/, leaving an aspiration, similar to English /h/, in its place: "los niños" [loh ní-ñoh]. The complete loss of the final /-s/, which is less frequent and less acceptable than the aspirated variety, will continue to have important consequences on the morphological structure of Spanish, as the language adapts to the loss of the plural morpheme on nouns and adjectives, and the informal second-person singular morpheme on verbs. For example, the mandatory use of the subject pronoun tú is one possible result of this development, since the verb ending in /-s/ is no longer available to mark the second person. The difficulty that this change causes to students of Spanish should not be underestimated. Their ability to comprehend dialects in which the /-s/ is aspirated or lost is greatly diminished in part because the /-s/ is such a frequent and significant morphological marker on verbs, nouns, and adjectives. However, students can be taught to pay attention to other morphological, syntactic, and contextual cues in the sentence, such as the third, person verb ending for plural subjects. For example, the phrase las niñas comen could be interpreted with a singular subject if pronounced without the final /-s/ of the article and noun, as in [la niña komen], except that the plural marker /-n/ indicates that the subject must be plural.

The confusion of syllable and word-final /-r/ and /-l/ in words such as parte [pálte], is found in Andalusia and in many areas of America, such as Chile, but it is most common in the Caribbean. Some authors have attributed this and other developments to the influence of African languages (Lipski 1994: 94-135), but the neutralization of these two liquids is common in other languages as well. This development is far less accepted than the aspiration or loss of /-s/, and seems to have a strong stigma attached to it.

The velarization of word-final /-n/, which is also common in Caribbean Spanish, results in a posterior shift in the point of articulation of the nasal from the alveolar region to the velar area. The resulting sound is similar to the "ng" of English, so that Spanish pan would be pronounced similar to English pong. This velarization is the first step in the weakening of the word-final nasal consonant. In some cases, the /-n/ is lost but the previous vowel becomes nasalized. This development is similar to what has already occurred in other Romance languages, such as French and Portuguese.

If we add to this list the weakening of word-final /-d/, as in libertad [libertá], which occurs frequently in all varieties of Spanish, it is evident that Spanish is following the course that many of the other Romance languages have already taken towards a word structure with open final syllables. In other words, the dialects that tend to eliminate word-final consonants are not corrupting the language, but instead are continuing a tendency that began in Latin. The preference towards the open final syllable in Spanish is also evident when one looks at borrowings from other languages, which are often pronounced without the final consonant, such as coñac pronounced as [ko-ñá].

While the goal of exposing our students to this and other phonological variation would not necessarily be to teach them to pronounce Spanish in this way, it would be very useful for them to be aware of this variation so that they can adjust to it and accept it more easily when coming into contact with speakers from these regions. Students often say that they cannot understand speakers from a given region, only because they have not had the opportunity to adapt to the variation that exists within that dialect. Word-final consonant loss within some dialects, such as those of the Caribbean, can be a major obstacle to comprehension if students are not aware of this variation. Moreover, the likelihood that our students will meet someone from the Caribbean in this country is much greater than that of meeting someone from Spain. Some students may wish to imitate this variation as well, just as other students may choose to imitate the Castilian "c,z," pronounced like the "th" in English think, or the Argentinian "y,ll," pronounced like the "s" in English measure, but this choice would be based on the dialect with which they have the most contact.

The Second-Person Subject Pronoun

As an example of morphological variation within Spanish, I would like to discuss the choice of the second-person subject pronoun in the Spanish-speaking world. While many textbooks continue to present the vosotros verbal paradigm to students, little or no attention is given to another second-person pronoun which is used by many more speakers than the Castilian vosotros. The vos form, which is used as an informal second-person singular pronoun in many regions of America, including Argentina and Central America, has survived in many regions of America despite its failure to be recognized as an acceptable alternative or addition to the standard tú/usted paradigm.

Many native speakers of Spanish, including those who use the vos form, believe that it is a derivation or corruption of the Castilian vosotros form. However, quite the opposite is true. Vos existed in medieval Spanish with two functions: as a formal second-person singular pronoun, alongside the informal tú, and as a second-person plural pronoun. A similar situation is still found in French, where vous is both a formal singular and a plural second-person pronoun. Over time, two changes began to take place in Spanish that altered the second-person pronoun system significantly. The singular vos became less and less formal, until it was viewed as the equivalent of Spanish tú. In addition, the plural vos was often accompanied by otros in order to clarify that this was the plural second-person pronoun (vos -"you" vs. vos otros -"you others"). A similar attempt is made in English to distinguish between the singular and plural you with expressions such as you all and you guys. The first change, where vos became informal, left a void in the place of the second-person formal pronoun, and this gap was filled by a new expression, vuestra merced, which reduced phonologically over time to usted. However, it is clear that singular vos was still in use when the Spaniards arrived in America, since vos has been maintained in many regions as a second-person singular informal pronoun.

Once again, one of the reasons for not teaching the vos verb forms to students is a practical one. Students already have a hard time distinguishing between the use of formal usted and informal tú in Spanish, so adding another pronoun to this would be difficult. However, there are many more speakers using vos than there are using vosotros, and textbooks continue to present this verb form. Another reason that the vos verb forms may not be presented is that there is little consistency from region to region, and several verb forms exist. For example, depending on the region, one might hear vos tomáis, with the diphthong of the original verb form, vos tomás, with reduction of the diphthong but retention of stress on the final syllable, or vos tomas, with the tú verb form (Paez Urdaneta 1981). The decision to use one pronoun over another varies considerably from region to region, from speaker to speaker, and from situation to situation as well. This variation makes it difficult to teach this form to our students, yet ignoring it completely seems inappropriate given the many regions in which it is used and the likelihood that our students will encounter this form at some point in their language careers.

The Third-Person Direct and Indirect Object Pronouns

As an example of the syntactic variation that exists in Spanish, I would like to turn to the use of the third-person direct and indirect object pronouns. Once again, I will return to a diachronic perspective to help explain the synchronic variation that exists today in Spanish.

An examination of the evolution of the Latin noun and pronoun system into the various Romance languages reveals a clear tendency towards the elimination of all case markings at the end of nouns. Classical Latin had six cases, which defined the syntactic function of nouns within a sentence. The nominative case marked nouns as subjects; the genitive marked possessors; the dative marked indirect objects; the accusative marked direct objects; the ablative marked adverbial functions such as "by, from, with, in, on"; and the vocative, which usually had the same form as the nominative, was used to address someone directly (Wheelock 1964: 6-7). In most of the Romance languages, the case system for nouns has been completely lost. The remaining noun forms usually derived from the accusative form of the Latin noun, and prepositions became used instead of case endings to indicate the syntactic function of the noun within a sentence. For example, the genitive case ending, which indicated the possessor, was replaced by the preposition de before the noun (ergo pre-position). In addition, word order became much more rigid than it was in Latin as the nominative (subject), dative (indirect object), and accusative (direct object) nouns began to occur more and more in a fixed position in relation to the verb. Although Spanish still enjoys a fair amount of flexibility in word order, the syntactic rules governing this order are much more rigid than they were in Latin, largely because of the loss of the case endings on nouns. The development of the ëpersonal aí before animate direct objects was also in response to the need to distinguish between an animate subject and an animate direct object when case endings were no longer available.

Within the pronoun system, the elimination of case markings has not been as complete. While Latin distinguished between nominative, genitive, dative, accusative, and ablative in all of the persons (first, second, third singular and plural), most of the Romance languages maintain a distinction only between the nominative (subject) pronouns and the object or oblique pronouns. In other words, the genitive, dative, accusative, and ablative cases have merged into one pronoun form. For example, Spanish uses the nominative or subject pronouns yo, tú, él, ella, usted, nosotros-as, vosotros-as, ellos-as, ustedes, and the object pronouns me, te, nos, os.

The one exception to this reduction is the third-person object pronouns, which continue to distinguish between the dative (indirect object) le, les, and the accusative (direct object) lo, la, los, las in Spanish. In some Romance languages, such as French (Harris 1988: 219) and Brazilian Portuguese (Parkinson 1988: 148), the distinction between these two cases has also been eliminated in the third-person pronoun, and one form is used for both direct and indirect object pronouns. In addition, there are some changes in Spanish which suggest that the distinction between direct and indirect object pronouns in the third person will someday be eliminated in some varieties of Spanish as well.

For several centuries, Spanish grammarians have noted the tendency in Castilian Spanish to use the third-person singular indirect object pronoun, le, to refer to masculine singular direct objects when the object is +human. An example of this leísmo can be found in response to the question ¿Has visto a Juan?, where one would respond with No, no le he visto, instead of the standard No, no lo he visto. This usage of le as a direct object pronoun in the singular has become so widespread in Castilian Spanish that the Real Academia has accepted it as an alternative to the standard lo form (Alarcos Llorach 1994: 202-204). Despite this acceptance, leísmo has not reached American Spanish to the same degree as in Spain, and lo continues to be used as the masculine singular direct object pronoun in most cases, while le is used as the singular indirect object pronoun.

In other regions of Spain, one finds even more variations in the use of third-person object pronouns. For example, laísmo refers to the use of the pronouns la and las for feminine indirect object pronouns, and loísmo implies the use of lo and los for masculine indirect object pronouns. Neither of these variations has reached the same level of acceptance as leísmo, yet their existence suggests an overall deterioration of what remains of the Latin case distinction in Spanish.

If we consider what the resulting pronoun system would look like if both leísmo and laísmo were to be used in both the singular and plural forms, we find a much simplified system, with distinctions in the third-person pronoun based on gender and humanness rather than case. Le/les would be used to refer to masculine humans, lo/los would be used to refer to masculine objects, and la/las would be used to refer to feminine humans or objects. A combination of loísmo and laísmo would be even simpler, since lo/los would be used for masculine objects, regardless of their human qualities, and la/las would refer to feminine objects and persons.

Despite the neatness of this hypothetical simplification, the complete elimination of the distinction between the direct object and indirect object pronoun in the third person is far from complete in Spanish. Yet once again this variation reflects the fact that Spanish, like any other language, is in a constant state of change. This change is normal and should be expected and accepted in any language as a viable alternative to the standard form. It is interesting to note that a nonstandard form, leísmo which has gained acceptance by the Real Academia, happens to occur as a variety in Castilian Spanish. It would be interesting to observe whether such an innovation in America would meet with the same degree of approval.

It is difficult to determine to what extent this syntactic variation should be taught to our students. The concept of direct and indirect object is difficult enough for students, since no distinction is made in English between these two cases. For example, the pronouns him and her are used both as direct and indirect objects: I saw him/her, I gave him/her the book. However, an awareness of this variation might be reassuring to students, since the development of leísmo, laísmo, and loísmo suggests that native speakers of Spanish are also having difficulties distinguishing between the direct and indirect object pronoun. It is also important for teachers to be aware of this variation, so that they can better understand and explain to their students when both lo and le sound acceptable to them.

The loss of the distinction between these two forms is due in large part to the fact that their functions are no longer distinguished in any other pronoun except for the third person. As Whitley points out, "Given such syncretism or convergence in marking, great pressure is exerted on the sole point where a distinction was inherited between dativo (IO) and acusativo (DO), namely, le(s) vs. lo(s) and la(s)" (1986: 173). The shift with each of these tendencies is away from pronouns that indicate case and towards pronouns that indicate gender, a feature that is quite commonly marked in Spanish nouns, pronouns, and adjectives.

Conclusion

Although the examples of language variation which were presented in this paper do not in any way cover all of the variation that exists in the Spanish-speaking world today, I chose these examples to demonstrate that the reasons for synchronic variation can usually be found in diachronic tendencies within a language or language family. The roots of all of these changes can be found within Latin, and a comparison of Spanish with other Romance languages often gives us insights into where Spanish may be heading. I also chose these examples to demonstrate that language is not stagnant. All of this variation exists because Spanish, like all other languages, is in flux, and it will continue to change and exhibit variation as long as it is a living, spoken language. Only dead languages remain the same, and if we want our students to have a full appreciation of Spanish as a living language, we must incorporate language variation into our curriculum.

Within the language classroom, exposure to this variation can benefit any student who will someday use the language in a real situation, outside of the classroom. For beginning students, most of this information would only cause more confusion, but advanced students have enough knowledge of the standard form to be prepared for some exposure to language variation. This exposure would help them to improve their processing skills, as they learn to listen for other cues in the input which will enable them to understand the message. To achieve this goal, authentic materials, such as news and television broadcasts, can be used in the classroom, but most of the language that is found in these materials is the standard form. Films from different countries tend to be a much better resource, since the language used is more authentic and less formal. Spanish speakers within the community are also an excellent resource, especially when students are given the opportunity to speak with this person one on one. Teachers can also record informal conversations between native speakers and have students listen to these recordings. However, the register of speech can vary dramatically depending on the situation that the speaker is in, and variation away from the standard form will only become evident when the speaker feels comfortable enough to speak in an informal register. Regardless of which materials are used to expose students to this variation, they will adapt much more easily to these differences if they are taught beforehand to listen to new cues that they may not have been aware of before. They will also gain an appreciation of the fact that there is not only one correct way to speak, and that even within the same language, a great deal of diversity exists.

References

Alarcos Llorach, Emilio. 1994. *Gramática de la lengua española.* Madrid: Espasa Calpe.

Barrutia, Richard, and Schwegler, Armin. 1992. *Fonética y fonología españolas,* 2nd ed. New York: John Wiley and Sons.

Canfield, Delos Lincoln. 1962. *La pronunciación del español en América.* Bogotá: Instituto Caro y Cuervo.

Harris, Martin, and Vincent, Nigel, eds. 1988. *The Romance Languages,* 2nd ed. New York: Oxford University Press.

Lipski, John. 1994. *Latin American Spanish.* New York: Longman.

Parkinson, Stephen. 1988. Portuguese. In Harris and Vincent, eds.: 131-169.

Paez Urdaneta, I. 1981. *Historia y geografía hispanoamericana del voseo.* Caracas: La Casa de Bello.

Wheelock, Frederic. 1964. *Latin,* 3rd ed. New York: Barnes and Noble.

Whitley, Melvin Stanley. 1986. *Spanish/English Contrasts.* Washington, D.C.: Georgetown University Press.